INSIDE
ANFIELD

Photographs

JOHN COCKS & ALAN WHYTE AT LIVERPOOL FOOTBALL CLUB and **ACTION IMAGES**

Design and Editorial

DESIGN/SECTION, FROME

First published in 1999 by

ANDRE DEUTSCH LIMITED

76 Dean Street, London W1V 5HA

www.vci.co.uk

For **LIVERPOOL FOOTBALL CLUB**

in association with **GRANADA MEDIA**

ISBN

0 233 99851 9

Reprographics by

RADSTOCK REPRODUCTIONS, BATH

Printed and bound in the UK by

BUTLER & TANNER LTD, FROME AND LONDON

INSIDE ANFIELD

LIFE AT LIVERPOOL FC

Paul Eaton

GRANADA
MEDIA

CONTENTS

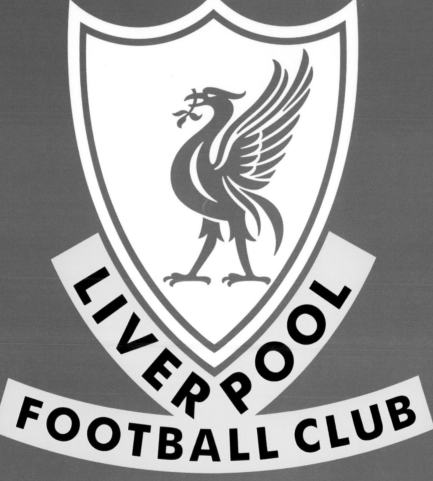

THE
GERARD HOULLIER

story

L iverpool manager Gérard Houllier always felt it was his destiny to coach in England – in the city where he first worked more than 30 years ago.

Despite never playing football at professional level, Houllier is one of the most highly respected coaches in the game and was a key figure in France's World Cup success in 1998.

But it could all have been so different for the Liverpool boss had he not convinced a small French club to hand him the chance to prove himself capable in football management.

Houllier began his working life as a schoolteacher teaching English in France, while at the same time turning out for his local amateur side Le Touquet-Paris-Plage. He even spent one year on Merseyside teaching at a Liverpool school to help him brush up on his English.

Houllier's first experience in football management came with his amateur team and he made a good enough impression to earn himself a chance coaching another small French team, Nœux Les Mines, a side in the French fifth division.

His success was instant and he took Nœux Les Mines to three successive promotions, straight into the second division. The footballing world took notice of this

The French League Championship trophy that Houllier won with PSG.

bright young manager, and he moved to Lens in 1982 where a much stiffer test and much greater expectations awaited him.

Again he proved himself a top class coach by taking Lens from fourteenth in the table to fifth in his first season in charge of the first division club. The following two seasons were not as successful and he endured the first real disappointments of his managerial career, although he still did enough to alert top French side Paris St-Germain to his abilities and he joined them in 1985.

Paris St-Germain had never won the League championship in their relatively short history, but that changed within one year of Houllier becoming boss and they celebrated wildly in 1986 as he led them to their first major triumph.

Upon arrival in England, Houllier quickly developed a reputation as a level-headed, calm and intelligent manager.

National call-up

This success led to his appointment as assistant to French football legend Michel Platini, who was then coach of the national team. After France's unsuccessful campaign in the 1992 European Championships Houllier was promoted to take sole control of the French team while Platini devoted all his efforts to working with the organising committee to ensure the 1998 World Cup finals were played in France.

Houllier's first qualifying campaign with France started brightly but turned into a nightmare. Having won five of their first six qualifying matches for USA '94 the team seemed well on their way to a comfortable qualification. However, having conceded a late equaliser to Sweden and having allowed Israel to come back from 2–1 down to beat them, France's World Cup fate was decided in the final match of the group against Bulgaria in Paris. With the scores level at 1–1 – a draw being enough to see the French qualify – Houllier's men needlessly lost possession in the dying stages of the game: Bulgaria's Kostadinov scored the winner.

Houllier was immensely disappointed and he resigned to work with the national coaching programme as a technical director. He coached many of the French youth teams and helped to develop the talents of players who went on to play a starring role in France's World Cup triumph in 1998.

Aimé Jacquet, France's manager during their successful World Cup campaign in 1998, admitted – after the Final victory over Brazil in Paris – that the French people owed a great deal of thanks to Houllier for the work he carried out behind the scenes.

Back to Merseyside

The World Cup over, Houllier's work with France was at an end and he was keen to return to club management. The chance to help revive Liverpool's fortunes was too tempting to resist. Despite reported approaches from Everton, Sheffield Wednesday and Glasgow Celtic, Houllier found the lure of Liverpool too tempting to resist and so returned to the city where he last worked 30 years ago.

After weeks of high-level talks, Houllier agreed to come to Liverpool in the role of joint manager alongside old Boot Room boy Roy Evans. History has shown that managerial pairings aren't successful but Evans and Houllier, with the unstinting backing of the Liverpool board, were desperate to prove people wrong and shared the belief that together they could make it work. The early signs were encouraging: after three matches of the 1998–99 season Liverpool topped the table after beating Newcastle United 4–1 convincingly at St James' Park. Gradually, though, results took a turn for the worse, culminating in a disastrous

Allez Les Bleus: Zinedine Zidane puts the home team 1–0 up in the 1998 World Cup Final.

run during November when the Reds lost three successive matches in front of their own supporters.

Speculation was rife that more changes would be made to the management staff and it was during that three-match losing sequence at Anfield that action was taken. A tearful Roy Evans announced he was to step down as joint team manager and so bring to an end more than 30 years of loyal service at Anfield. His assistant Doug Livermore also left the club to make way for Gérard Houllier's new management team.

Old and new

Anfield old boy Phil Thompson was both surprised and delighted to get the call to be Houllier's number two, while the rest of the coaching staff comprised Patrice Bergues, a longtime friend of Houllier's from France, Sammy Lee and goalkeeping coach Joe Corrigan.

Liverpool fans were already familiar with Thompson as he not only managed the reserve side during the early Nineties, but was also a player of great distinction with the club, captaining them to European Cup glory in 1981 in Paris.

Sammy Lee and Joe Corrigan are also familiar names to Reds fans as they have been involved in the Anfield set-up for a number of years. Frenchman Patrice Bergues was a new name to many, though, when he arrived at Anfield to join the coaching staff following Houllier's appointment as joint manager. Bergues began his career as a non-professional midfielder with French side Nœux Les Mines – previously coached by Houllier – before succeeding Houllier as coach of Lens. He then joined up with the Liverpool boss at the French Football Federation and jumped at the chance to join Houllier again at Anfield.

TOP: Happy days: Liverpool's first foray into joint managership gets off to a flying start in 1998. The team were soon top of the Premier League, but it was not to last...
MIDDLE: As the club's results declined, Roy Evans resigned in November 1998.
BOTTOM: The Boss: Houllier discusses tactics with some of his players.

The remainder of the 1998–99 season was a non-event in many ways for the Reds and the summer break couldn't come quickly enough for Houllier so that he could go about reshaping the Liverpool squad in his own way.

Having already signed defender Rigobert Song from Italian side Salernitana and young French talent Djimi Traore from Laval, Houllier knew he needed to strengthen further and wasted no time during the summer in bringing in reinforcements for the new campaign.

In total seven new players arrived in the 1999 off-season, all foreign and many of them unknown to Liverpool fans. Goalkeeper Sander Westerveld, defenders Sami Hyypia and Stephane Henchoz, midfielders Dietmar Hamann and Vladimir Smicer and strikers Erik Meijer and Titi Camara all arrived at a total cost of approximately £25m.

Westerveld became the most expensive goalkeeper in British football when he signed for a reported £4m, Hamann became Liverpool's second most expensive player of all time at a cost of £8m while Titi Camara became the first Guinean international to play in the Premiership.

The Liverpool boss received much criticism for his apparent obsession with signing foreigners, but he revealed that significant bids had also been made for Englishmen during the summer: in all cases the offers were rejected.

Nonetheless he brushed aside all criticism of his foreign signings by simply declaring: 'Their country is Liverpool and their language is football.'

He retained the English backbone of the side, though, with new captain Jamie Redknapp and new vice-captain Robbie Fowler assuming more responsibility and with the maturing Michael Owen, Jamie

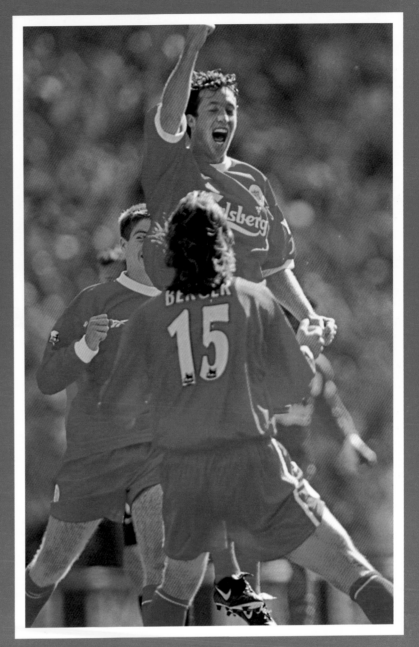

On top of the world: Robbie Fowler celebrates with his team mates after he scored the first goal against Arsenal in the Reds' 2–0 victory. Fowler has a great record against the Gunners.

Carragher, Dominic Matteo, Steven Gerrard and David Thompson all set to play important roles in Liverpool's future.

With the construction of Liverpool's Soccer Academy in Kirkby, Houllier can rest assured that the excellent production line of Liverpool youngsters itching for a first team chance will continue well into the new millennium.

Ins and outs

Many players have arrived at Anfield since Houllier took sole control, but just as many have left as the club has attempted to balance the books. With Rob Jones released at the end of last season on a free transfer, Houllier set about selling the fringe players at Anfield or those he thought had no part to play in his red revolution.

Steve McManaman was an exception – he would have had a big part to play in Houllier's plans – but decided to make the break and look for a new career abroad. He eventually joined Spanish giants Real Madrid on a free transfer under the Bosman ruling.

The old and the new... Anfield favourite Michael Owen comes on for Titi Camara during Liverpool's 2–0 victory over Arsenal in August 1999. Gérard Houllier looks on.

Undoubtedly the biggest surprise was Houllier's sale of Paul Ince to Middlesbrough for £1m. David James (Aston Villa), Oyvind Leonhardsen (Tottenham), Sean Dundee (Stuttgart), Jean-Michel Ferri (Sochaux), Jason McAteer (Blackburn), Bjorn Kvarme (St Etienne), Karl-Heinz Riedle (Fulham), Steve Harkness (Benfica) and Tony Warner (Millwall) also headed for the Anfield exit door.

With expectations high at the beginning of another season, Liverpool made the perfect start by winning at Hillsborough against Sheffield Wednesday thanks to goals from Robbie Fowler and Titi Camara. Disappointments followed with defeats by both Middlesbrough and newly-promoted Watford, but the Reds were soon back on track by defeating title contenders Leeds United at Elland Road and Arsenal at Anfield in the space of five days. But as Liverpool discovered last year, the Premiership is a long, hard season and nothing is gained by reading too much into early-season form.

The future...

This is a key season for Gérard Houllier: his first full English League campaign in sole control. The man who first discovered the magic of Anfield while a teacher more than 30 years ago is charged with the responsibility of taking Liverpool back to the top of the English game – and few would bet against him once again achieving his goals.

Houllier in brief

1973–76	Player-coach for Le Touquet-Paris-Plage
1976–82	Head coach and manager of Nœux Les Mines, winning promotion from fifth to second division
1982–85	Coach of Lens
1985–1988	Coach of Paris St-Germain. Won French League title in 1986
1988	Takes over as technical director of French national team, assistant to coach Michel Platini and responsible for coaching at all levels of international youth football
July 9, 1992	Takes over from Platini as France coach
August 26, 1992	First match as coach against Brazil in a friendly at Parc des Princes
September 9, 1992	France kick off qualifying campaign for 1994 World Cup, losing 2–0 to Bulgaria in Sofia
October 13, 1993	France lose 3–2 to Israel in World Cup qualifier at Parc des Princes
November 17, 1993	France lose 2–1 to Bulgaria at Parc des Princes, failing to qualify for 1994 World Cup after 90th-minute goal by Emil Kostadinov
November 25, 1993	Houllier resigns as coach after 12 internationals (7 wins, 1 draw, 4 defeats), but remains as technical director
1996	Head coach of French under-18 team who become European champions
1997	Head coach of French under-20 team which reached quarter-finals of World Championship
July 12, 1998	France win the World Cup
July 16, 1998	Appointed joint team manager of Liverpool
November 12, 1998	Appointed sole manager of Liverpool following the resignation of Roy Evans

Anfield Stadium has not only played host to many of the game's finest players; it is also the home of one of the world's most famous clubs.

Liverpool's domination of the English game throughout the Seventies and Eighties ensured that there were many glorious days and nights at Anfield as the club's supporters celebrated a succession of trophies which came to reside on Merseyside.

It may come as a shock to some to learn that it was Everton, Liverpool's arch-rivals, who first played their home matches at Anfield and had there not been a dispute over rent, the Toffees could still be playing their home games at the famous stadium even today.

It was back in 1884 when Everton started playing at Anfield and they continued to do so for eight years, until a major row erupted concerning Everton's renting of the land. A dispute with John Houlding, the owner of the land, led to Everton leaving Anfield to purchase another site in the area, known as Goodison Park.

At that time Anfield was regularly attracting 8,000 supporters for games, and John Houlding had ploughed a lot of his own money into transforming the stadium into one worthy of a local football team. A small stand had been erected to house the fans, but with Everton gone the stadium was empty and Houlding was out of pocket.

dry during bad weather. At the time it was the largest stand in the country. The top mast of the ship *Great Eastern* was taken from the breaker's yard in Rock Ferry and was erected alongside the Kop, where it remains today.

In 1957 Anfield had floodlights installed, enabling the team to play in the evening. They were used for the first time on October 30 for a game against Everton which was staged to commemorate the 75th anniversary of the Liverpool County Football Association.

In 1963 the board of directors agreed to spend approximately £350,000 on a new stand on the Kemlyn Road side of the ground. It was a cantilevered stand able to hold 6,700 supporters. Soon after, major alterations were also made to the Anfield Road End as that stand too was turned into a large, covered standing area.

One of the biggest and most exciting redevelopments came in 1973 when the Main Stand was reduced to rubble and a new, smarter stand was constructed in its place. It was officially opened by the Duke of Kent on March 10, 1973 and still stands at Anfield today.

The birth of LFC...

As a result he made the decision to form his own team to play at Anfield – Liverpool Football Club. Their first match was played on Thursday September 1, 1892 against Rotherham. It was a friendly encounter which Liverpool won 7–1.

Following a successful first season in the Lancashire League, Liverpool were granted permission to play in the Football League and the first national League game at Anfield was played against Lincoln City on September 9, 1893. Liverpool won 4–0 in front of 5,000 supporters.

With interest in the club growing all the time and with attendances on the increase, a new stand was erected in 1895 to seat 3,000 fans. It was built on the site of the present Main Stand and was used until 1973, although alterations and renovations were made to it as the years passed by.

Another new stand was constructed in 1903 at the Anfield Road End. It was made from timber and corrugated iron. When Liverpool won their second League title in 1906 the directors rewarded the fans by

building a banked terrace at the Walton Breck Road End. Local journalist Ernest Edwards from the *Liverpool Daily Post and Echo* christened it the Spion Kop after a hill in South Africa where a local regiment had suffered heavy losses during the Boer War.

The next major improvement to Anfield came in 1928, when the Kop was redesigned to house 30,000 fans. A huge roof was erected to keep the supporters

The Kop: Liverpool fans are famous the world over for their unstinting vocal support.

ABOVE: *Remembrance: The memorial to the Hillsborough disaster of 1989 attracts tributes from thousands of true football fans from clubs around the world. BELOW: The 96 victims are named.*

iron gates with the simple but powerful message 'You'll Never Walk Alone' across the top. They were named The Shankly Gates and were officially opened by his widow Nessie.

Following the Hillsborough tragedy, a memorial was constructed beside the Shankly Gates. An eternal flame flickers in remembrance of the 96, whose names are listed down two columns on the memorial. Flowers and scarves are regularly draped by its side from supporters everywhere who were shocked and saddened by the disaster.

A second tier was added to the Kemlyn Road Stand in the early Nineties at a cost of £10m, and for the first time executive boxes and dining lounges were seen at the stadium. The stand was now able to hold 11,000 fans and was renamed the Centenary Stand in celebration of Liverpool's hundred years of playing football at Anfield.

The biggest change of all was still to come: following the Hillsborough disaster of 1989, where 96 Liverpool fans lost their lives, Lord Justice Taylor had issued instructions that all top division clubs must have all-seater stadiums – to prevent another Hillsborough-type tragedy. For Liverpool this meant the end of the world-famous Spion Kop where thousands of fanatical Reds fans turned up week after week in support of their team.

In May 1994 after Liverpool's final match of the season – against Norwich City –

work began to demolish the Kop. A splendid 12,000-seater stand was built in its place. It was the biggest single-tier stand in Europe. Many tears were shed as fans left the Kop for the last time, and there was a dash for souvenirs as fans were desperate to get their hands on any kind of memento to remind them of their times in the middle of a noisy, swaying, flag-waving Kop.

Further reconstruction of Anfield continued in 1997 when the Anfield Road stand was transformed into a two-tier stand, which brought Anfield's capacity to over 45,000, making it the second biggest club stadium in the country, behind Manchester United's Old Trafford.

Outside the stadium there have also been changes over the years. Following the sad death of former Liverpool manager Bill Shankly, the club decided to honour his memory by erecting a set of wrought-

Previous managers

More recently a bronze statue of Bill Shankly has been erected in front of the Kop Grandstand. The statue was designed and crafted by local sculptor Tom Murphy. It stands 7'6" high and weighs three- quarters of a ton. The message on the statue reads simply 'He made the people happy'.

Bob Paisley, Liverpool's most successful-ever manager, is the most recent to be honoured with the opening of the 'Paisley Gateway' which leads on to the Kop forecourt. Three European Cups – reflecting Paisley's historic achievement as Liverpool boss – are depicted on the top of the gates while the coat of arms for Liverpool and that for Hetton-le-Hole, his birthplace, are inscribed on the gates.

Anfield has changed dramatically over the years to keep pace with the popularity of football and strict safety demands. These days it is common for home matches to be sold out weeks in advance. Having already staged international matches during Euro 96, it has been listed as one of the stadiums the Football Association would use should England be elected to host the World Cup in 2006.

The Glory of Anfield:
ABOVE and BELOW:
The pitch on a match day
and when empty; RIGHT:
The famous sign that
opponents from around
the world fear.

A Graham Carter (kit manager)
2 Stephane Henchoz
16 Dietmar Hamann
22 Titi Camara
13 Karlheinz Riedle (now Fulham)
1 Sander Westerveld
26 Jorgen Nielsen
29 Stephen Wright
6 Phil Babb
14 Vegard Heggem
20 Stig Inge Bjornebye
J Garry Armer (masseur)
B Joe Corrigan (goalkeeping coach)
C Patrice Bergues (coach)
5 Steve Staunton
31 Frode Kippe
7 Vladimir Smicer
15 Patrik Berger
4 Rigobert Song
3 Bjorn Tore Kvarme (now St Etienne)
32 Jon Newby
18 Erik Meijer
12 Sami Hyypia
30 Djimi Traore
27 Haukur Ingi Gudnason
D Phil Thompson (assistant manager)
E Sammy Lee (coach)
25 David Thompson
24 Danny Murphy
28 Steven Gerrard
11 Jamie Redknapp (captain)
F Gérard Houllier (team manager)
9 Robbie Fowler (vice captain)
21 Dominic Matteo
23 Jamie Carragher
10 Michael Owen

Phil Babb

Patrik Berger

Stig Bjornebye

Titi Camara

Jamie Carragher

Robbie Fowler

Brad Friedel

	HEIGHT	SOURCE	PLACE OF BIRTH	DATE OF BIRTH	SQUAD NUMBER
Phil Babb	6'	Coventry City	Lambeth	30.11.70	6
Patrik Berger	6'1"	Borussia Dortmund	Prague	10.11.73	15
Stig Bjornebye	5'10"	Rosenborg	Elverum	11.12.69	20
Titi Camara	6'	Marseille	Donka	17.11.72	22
Jamie Carragher	6'1"	Trainee	Liverpool	28.1.78	23
Robbie Fowler	5'11"	Trainee	Liverpool	9.4.75	9
Brad Friedel	6'3"	Columbus Crew	Ohio	18.5.71	19

Steven Gerrard

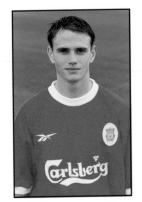
Haukur Gudnason

Dietmar Hamann

Vegard Heggem

Stephane Henchoz

Sami Hyypia

Dominic Matteo

	HEIGHT	SOURCE	PLACE OF BIRTH	DATE OF BIRTH	SQUAD NUMBER
Steven Gerrard	6'1"	Trainee	Liverpool	30.5.80	28
Haukur Gudnason	5'10"	Keflavik	Keflavik	8.9.78	27
Dietmar Hamann	6'2"	Newcastle Utd	Waldasson	27.8.73	16
Vegard Heggem	5'11"	Rosenborg	Trondheim	13.7.75	14
Stephane Henchoz	6'1"	Blackburn Rovers	Billens	7.9.74	2
Sami Hyypia	6'4"	Willem II	Porvoo	7.10.73	12
Dominic Matteo	6'1"	Trainee	Dumfries	24.4.74	21

Erik Meijer

Danny Murphy

Jorgen Nielsen

Michael Owen

Jamie Redknapp

Vladimir Smicer

	HEIGHT	SOURCE	PLACE OF BIRTH	DATE OF BIRTH	SQUAD NUMBER
Erik Meijer	6'2"	Bayer Leverkusen	Meersen	2.8.69	18
Danny Murphy	5'9"	Crewe Alexandra	Chester	18.3.77	24
Jorgen Nielsen	6'	Hvidovre	Nykabing	6.5.71	26
Michael Owen	5'8"	Trainee	Chester	14.12.79	10
Jamie Redknapp	6'	Bournemouth	Barton-on-Sea	25.6.73	11
Vladimir Smicer	5'10"	RC Lens	Degin	24.5.73	7

Rigobert Song

Steve Staunton

David Thompson

Djimi Traore

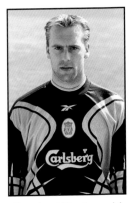
Sander Westerveld

Stephen Wright

	HEIGHT	SOURCE	PLACE OF BIRTH	DATE OF BIRTH	SQUAD NUMBER
Rigobert Song	6'	Salernitana	Nkenlicock	1.7.76	4
Steve Staunton	6'1"	Aston Villa	Drogheda	19.1.69	5
David Thompson	5'7"	Trainee	Birkenhead	12.9.77	25
Djimi Traore	6'3"	Laval	Saint-Ouen	1.3.80	30
Sander Westerveld	6'4"	Vitesse Arnhem	Enschede	23.10.74	1
Stephen Wright	6'	Trainee	Liverpool	8.2.80	29

ENGLAND

Phil Babb

Jamie Carragher

Robbie Fowler

Steven Gerrard

Danny Murphy

Jon Newby

Michael Owen

Jamie Redknapp

David Thompson

Stephen Wright

This map shows the countries of origin of the current Liverpool squad. Please note that it does not show countries that players may have played for in international matches.

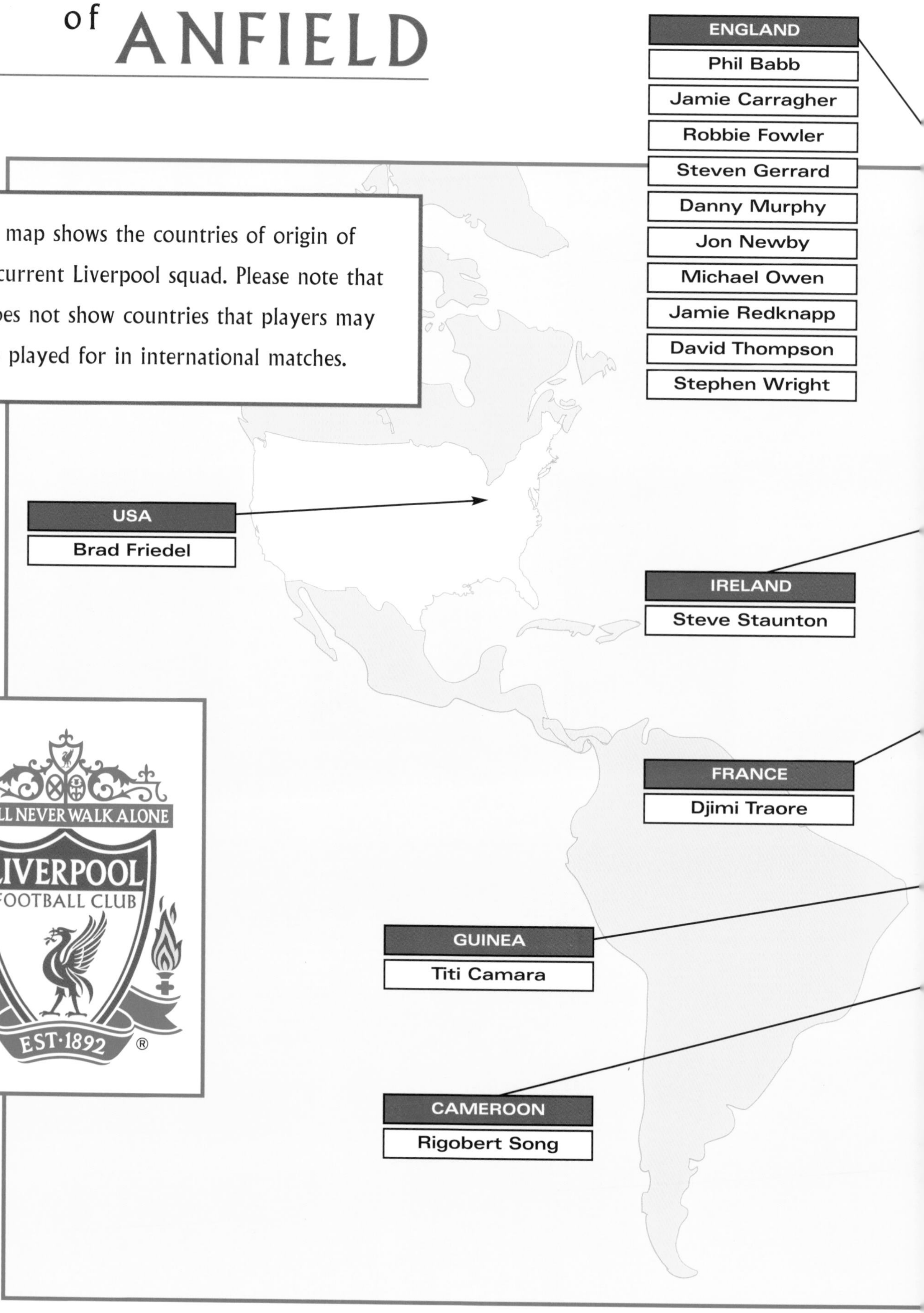

USA

Brad Friedel

IRELAND

Steve Staunton

YOU'LL NEVER WALK ALONE

LIVERPOOL
FOOTBALL CLUB

EST·1892 ®

FRANCE

Djimi Traore

GUINEA

Titi Camara

CAMEROON

Rigobert Song

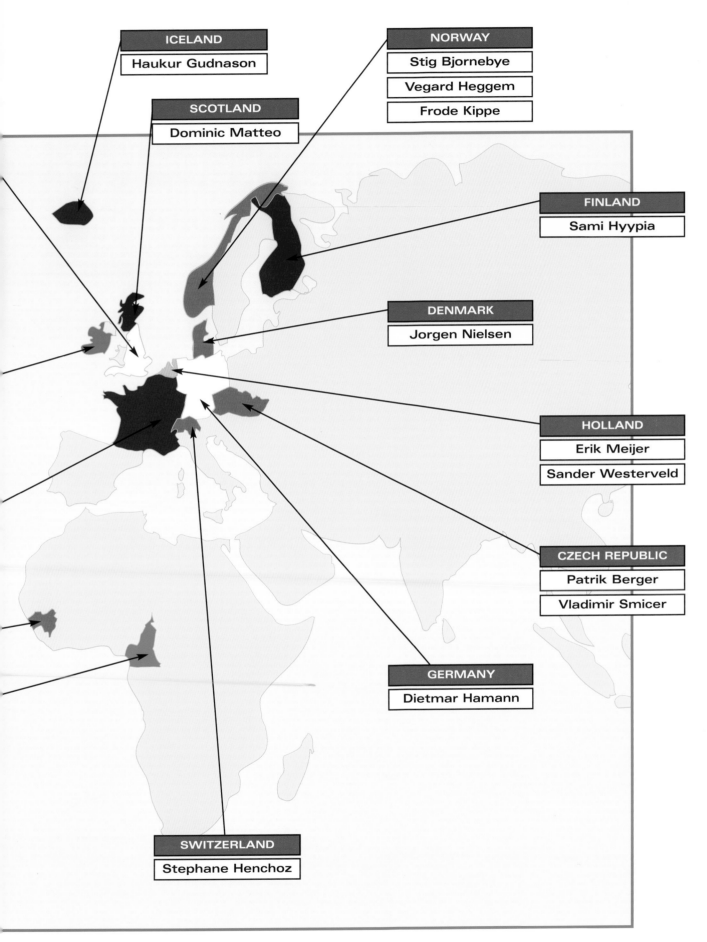

ICELAND

Haukur Gudnason

NORWAY

Stig Bjornebye

Vegard Heggem

Frode Kippe

SCOTLAND

Dominic Matteo

FINLAND

Sami Hyypia

DENMARK

Jorgen Nielsen

HOLLAND

Erik Meijer

Sander Westerveld

CZECH REPUBLIC

Patrik Berger

Vladimir Smicer

GERMANY

Dietmar Hamann

SWITZERLAND

Stephane Henchoz

Titi Camara
From Africa to Anfield

PLAYER STATS

Date of birth	November 17, 1972
Birthplace	Donka (Guinea)
Position	Striker
Height	6'
Signed	July 1999
From	Marseille (France)
Fee	£2.6m

Guinean star Titi Camara has only been on Merseyside for a matter of months, but already he has made enough friends to ensure he will be happy at Liverpool for many years to come.

Camara immediately endeared himself to the Liverpool fans with a storming start to his Anfield career which saw him score two goals in the opening five games of the season to leave manager Gérard Houllier delighted with his £2.6m striking acquisition.

Camara is the first player from Guinea to play in the Premiership but the early signs are that his unpredictable but effective style will be exciting Liverpool fans throughout the season.

He isn't particularly interested in personal achievements, though. He wants to help bring the glory days back to Anfield – glory days he remembers well from afar.

He says: 'Liverpool Football Club is mythical. They have won everything and done everything and for me to be part of the scene at Anfield now is very exciting. I know all about what Liverpool have achieved in the past and all the players here now have a responsibility to bring the same kind of success back to the club. I am aware of the pressures on us because I have seen the Liverpool sides of old and I know how good they were, but there is no reason why we can't enjoy some success of our own. We have an embarrassment of riches in our squad and everywhere you look you will see a top-class international player. We all have individual goals to aim for as well as a collective team goal. If we play to our potential then we can realise all of our dreams.'

Stunning welcome

Of course the dreams of the players are shared by Liverpool fans all over the world and Camara admits he was overcome by the reception he received when he first appeared in the Premiership.

He says: 'Our first match was at Sheffield

Wednesday and when I ran on to the field I saw the national flag of Guinea draped over the stands where the Liverpool fans were sat. That took my breath away and made me even more determined to prove myself as a Liverpool player. I want to win for those fans who have been so good to me and who are so important to the fortunes of this team.

'I have a lot to learn about English football before I can really say I am used to it but I am encouraged by the way I have settled so far. I keep saying it, but the speed of the game here is very fast and you rarely get time to settle for too long on the ball. As a striker you get no time at all to control the ball and then look to pass it to a team-mate – everything is very hurried and that is why you need to have a good first touch.

Different world

'Strikers aren't protected by referees anywhere near as much as they are in France because over here physical contact is an important part of the game. I have belief in my ability, though, and I am sure I will be able to adapt given time.'

Camara made the best possible start to his Liverpool career with a debut goal at Hillsborough before scoring one of the goals of the season so far, during the Reds' magnificent victory at Leeds United. He simply says: 'I am a striker and so I have to score goals. Just because I have some under my belt doesn't mean that I have done enough now, though.

'I have to keep working hard, keep improving and keep hitting the back of the net. I can't say my season has been a success because of the goal at Leeds. That was one game which now is in the past. I know people have high expectations of me but I have high expectations of myself as well.

'This may be a different challenge for me but it is one I am relishing and Liverpool fans can rest assured that I will always give my all for them and for the club.'

Camara is doubtless going to have to get used to the price of fame if his promising start to the season continues as it has begun. He may be an unfamiliar face to many at the moment – but that could easily change very quickly.

He says: 'The big difference between being here and being at my previous club Marseille is that I can go out around Liverpool without always being recognised. That suits me perfectly because I'm not the sort of person to court the limelight. As long as I am doing well on the field and everybody from the manager to the fans is happy with me then I will be very content.'

Titi Camara has fitted in well with Robbie Fowler (left) and the rest of the Liverpool team.

Dietmar Hamann
Midfield Dynamite

PLAYER STATS

Date of birth	August 27, 1973
Birthplace	Waldasson (Germany)
Position	Midfielder
Height	6'2"
Signed	July 1999
From	Newcastle United
Fee	£8m

German midfielder Dietmar Hamann is looking to make up for lost time as he gets set to kick off his Liverpool career.

Liverpool's most expensive summer signing suffered opening day misery at Sheffield Wednesday when he sustained ankle ligament damage which ruled him out of the opening months of the season.

But having regained full fitness Hamann is ready to show the Liverpool fans why Gérard Houllier spent £8m to bring him from Newcastle to Liverpool. He insists the transfer fee will not weigh on his shoulders.

He says: 'These days the market dictates the transfer fees. In a couple of years' time we could well be seeing transfers of £20m taking place regularly. On the other hand the prices could fall; we just don't know what will happen. My transfer fee is no burden on me, though, whatsoever. If I play well then no-one will have any reason to question the amount of money Liverpool

spent on me. The important thing is to play good football, win games and enjoy some success. That is our aim this season.

'I came to Liverpool because I am impressed with their ambitions and I am convinced that we have a squad capable of doing very well. We have a very young squad and all the lads get on really well together which is extremely important.'

Premiership rivals Arsenal wanted to sign Hamann, as did Borussia Dortmund from his native Germany, but the 24-year-old midfielder couldn't resist the opportunity to join Gérard Houllier's Anfield revolution.

He says: 'I made my mind up in the summer that I was going to leave Newcastle and they told me I would be allowed to leave if any interested club

offered an acceptable fee. There was an offer from Arsenal and I also knew that Liverpool and Borussia Dortmund were interested in me.

'I didn't really fancy a move back to Germany. I enjoyed my one season in the Premiership with Newcastle and so didn't want to leave England. I was always tempted towards Liverpool and now I am delighted to be here. You never know how many times in a career a chance will come for you to play at one of the biggest clubs in Europe. I couldn't turn this offer down.'

Many attractions

There were several factors which contributed to Hamann's desire to remain in England – not least the honesty in Premiership football. He says: 'In the

Premiership there is no diving and other players don't want to deliberately get you booked by the referee. If you are fouled then you get up, shake hands and play on. That is a terrific attitude to have and reflects well on the game in this country.

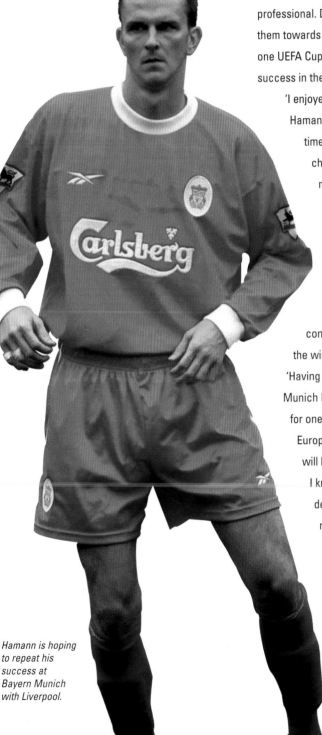

Hamann is hoping to repeat his success at Bayern Munich with Liverpool.

'I also love the way the fans get behind their team. They very rarely get on the backs of their own players even when things aren't going too well. The atmosphere inside English grounds is very special and it wasn't something that I wanted to lose from my career.'

Before his move to Newcastle United, Hamann spent ten years with Bayern Munich in Germany, five of them as a professional. During that time he helped them towards two league titles (1994, 1997), one UEFA Cup victory (1996) and also success in the German Cup (1998).

'I enjoyed my time in Munich,' says Hamann. 'But there always comes a time when you are ready for a change. I felt that I needed to make a move and to try something else and that is why I went to Newcastle. It was a pity that we didn't have more success last season at St James' Park but I am very confident I will be able to taste the winning feeling again at Anfield. 'Having played for so long at Bayern Munich I know what it is like to play for one of the biggest clubs in Europe and that is why I am sure I will have no problems at Liverpool. I know and understand the demands of the fans and I realise the expectations which come with playing for a massive club. Liverpool may not have had the best of times lately but there is no doubting they are still one of the biggest clubs around and it is only going to be a matter of time

before we are at the top again.'

But the big question that all Liverpool fans want answering ahead of another Anfield season is whether Gérard Houllier's new-look Reds side can jump from the seventh place finish of last season to the number one spot in just one year.

Says Hamann: 'That might be asking a bit much but we will certainly be giving it everything we have. We can definitely do better than seventh place. I think we have to aim for the top five and then hope we can build from there as the season goes on. It would be great to secure a top three finish and qualify for the Champions League next year but to do that would mean a season of consistency and in order to give everybody confidence that we could achieve that, it is vital that we make a good start.

'There is no doubt that helping Liverpool become the best in England again is going to be one of the biggest challenges of my career. We have a very good squad of players, all of whom can do a good job for the team when called upon. I like the attitude of the manager and his knowledge of the game is first-class. As long as we stick together throughout the season then I believe we will do well.'

Hamann, whose wife gave birth to their second child a couple of months ago, is looking forward to welcoming his family to the city of Liverpool.

He says: 'It was hard at first because they were in Munich and I was in Liverpool, but we did keep in touch as much as possible. It will be better when they are over here and we have found somewhere to live. I haven't seen too much of the city so far but what I have seen I have liked. The fans have been very welcoming to me as well which is always nice and I hope I can strike up a good relationship with them over the coming months at Anfield.'

Sami Hyypia
The Famous Finn

PLAYER STATS

Date of birth	October 7, 1973
Birthplace	Porvoo (Finland)
Position	Central Defender
Height	6'4"
Signed	June 1999
From	Willem II
Fee	£2.6m

Giant defender Sami Hyypia has not only made a big name for himself in England following his magnificent early season Liverpool form – he has also increased his popularity dramatically in Finland!

The Finnish international has been one of his country's better players over the last few years, but his move to Anfield and subsequent excellent displays at the heart of the Reds' defence have all but led to him becoming a national hero back home.

He says: 'I have heard stories from Finland that people are very proud of what I have done and that is pleasing. I love my country and it is nice that people over there respect me for what I am doing on the field. I have done a number of interviews with Finnish journalists since my move to Liverpool and everybody seems to be very excited with the fact that I am playing in the Premiership.'

Liverpool supporters may not have been familiar with the name Sami Hyypia when Gérard Houllier snapped him up, but the early signs are encouraging that Houllier now has the personnel to cure the club's persistent defensive problems.

Says Sami: 'I knew when I came over here that Liverpool had been struggling in the League for a while and people told me they had problems in defence. I saw it as a great challenge for me to come here and play my part in helping them out. I don't know what the problem has been in the past but I am sure we can all sort it out together. I can offer Liverpool many attributes with my game and so far I think I have settled well into the Premiership.'

Sami's height and presence combined with Jamie Carragher's experience has led to a promising partnership developing between two players whose best footballing years still lie ahead of them.

'Playing alongside Jamie is good for me because he talks a lot and that is something I needed during my first few months at Liverpool,' says Sami. 'He knows the Premiership better than I do and his experience will help me out. We are constantly talking during games so that we each know what the other one is doing and, although there have been some mistakes made, I do feel we will get better and better as the games go by.

'There are lots of other defenders here as well, of course, and it is important that the players in the team continue to perform otherwise the manager will be within his rights to make changes. I am in the side at the moment and I would dearly love to stay there.'

Unexpected

As with all foreigners experiencing the Premiership for the first time Sami admits several surprises lay in store for him when he made his Liverpool debut, but thankfully there was nothing he felt he couldn't cope with.

He explains: 'I have never been involved in football matches played at such a pace in my life and it is frightening at times. The game never stops for 90 minutes and there is no time to take a breather. The football is very exciting, though, and I can see why it is so popular all over Europe. You don't get too many bad games and that must be good from the point of view of the fans.

'The strikers are much more physical as well in this country and so for me to be able to deal with them I have to become more aggressive at times. I enjoy a challenge and a battle though so I am really enjoying myself on the field. Once I have had time to completely adapt to the Premiership then I will be fine.

'I started my career playing in Finland where the standard isn't great and the game is played at a relatively slow pace. Then I moved to Holland which was a step up from Finland but still it doesn't really prepare you for English football. The standard of play in Holland is good and I am sure my game improved during my time with Willem II, but playing for Liverpool is a different matter entirely.'

Hyypia captained Willem II to second place in last season's Dutch league, thereby ensuring them qualification for this season's Champions League.

He says: 'I have given up the chance to play in the Champions League to sign for Liverpool but that was a decision I felt I had to make. Besides, I wouldn't have come here if I didn't honestly believe this club would soon be in the Champions League as well. That is what we are all aiming for and I am confident that, with the quality of players we have here, we will soon be achieving success and competing with the best in Europe.'

Sami Hyypia in action against Wolverhampton Wanderers in a pre-season friendly.

Erik Meijer
Challenging for a Place

PLAYER STATS	
Date of birth	August 2, 1969
Birthplace	Meerssen (Holland)
Position	Striker
Height	6'2"
Signed	June 1999
From	Bayer Leverkusen (Germany)
Fee	Free transfer

By his own admission striker Erik Meijer has taken a gamble coming to Liverpool and trying to dislodge England men Robbie Fowler and Michael Owen from the first team.

He is realistic enough to know that when fit, Fowler and Owen will play but he realises the need for different options in the modern game and he is hoping that his powerful forward play will soon see him fulfil his dream of playing for Liverpool.

He says: 'I'm not daft and I know that Robbie Fowler and Michael Owen are world-class players who will play when they are fit. That makes common sense because any manager in the world would love to have them in their team.

'People have either said that I am taking a big gamble with my career or that I am just mad. I see it as an exciting challenge for me and it is one I am relishing. All the way through my career I have had to work hard to achieve success because perhaps

there have been other players at my club who were ahead of me. For that reason I worked as hard as I could day in and day out to improve my skills and that is what has got me here today.

'I understand it is not possible for everybody to play every week but I hope I will get a chance at some point during the season. I am taller than the other strikers which obviously gives the manager a different option if he decided to alter the tactics for a particular game. Liverpool haven't had that alternative for a while and so I know the door is open for me here.'

Meijer was the first of Liverpool's seven new signings to put pen to paper on his Anfield deal after agreeing to a Bosman-style move from previous club Bayer

Leverkusen at the start of the year.

'This is a dream move for me because Liverpool are such a massive club who command ultimate respect throughout the footballing world. I could have signed a new contract in Germany with Bayer Leverkusen and I also know that Borussia Dortmund were interested in signing me, but I felt that this was an exciting time to be joining Liverpool because there are a lot of fresh faces and I want to be a part of something big and successful here.

'I played for four years in the Bundesliga and I thought I did quite well during that time. There were many other German clubs who wanted to sign me but once I heard of Liverpool's interest it was an easy decision for me to make.

'I have enjoyed my early months on Merseyside and I haven't for one second regretted my decision to come over here. Of course I would have liked to play more on the field but if I keep working hard and doing well for the reserves then that situation will eventually take care of itself.'

United nations

The influx of continental stars heading to Anfield led to criticism from people who are concerned about the amount of foreign players coming into the Premiership. Meijer is adamant that good players should always be welcome, and he cites his experiences earlier in his career as a good example.

He says: 'At Bayer Leverkusen we had four Croatians, three Brazilians, two Poles as well as players from Holland and the Czech Republic. They were good players who improved our side which meant that the quality of football in our league was of a higher standard as well. That team is in the Champions League this season which shows that they must be doing something right. I know that English people would like English players in their team but Liverpool did attempt to sign British players without any success.

'I am sure that if we are successful on the field over the next couple of seasons then no Liverpool fans will mind who is in the team. Besides, there is still a healthy crop of local lads as well which I know is always important to local fans.'

The well-documented quote that 'Our country is Liverpool and our language is football' perfectly sums up the spirit and camaraderie in the Anfield camp and Meijer is confident that all the new boys will prove to be quality additions to the squad.

He says: 'I don't feel like a foreigner here because I am adapting and attempting to fit in with the Liverpool way of doing things. It has to be like that otherwise it won't work. All the lads here are determined to integrate themselves into the Liverpool way and that can only be a good thing.'

Meijer's best performance so far came when he scored two goals in September's Worthington Cup tie at Hull City.

Vladimir Smicer
Raring to Go

Czech star Vladimir Smicer is convinced the 'good atmosphere' within Anfield will ultimately lead the Reds to success in the future.

PLAYER STATS

Date of birth	May 24, 1973
Birthplace	Degin (Czech Republic)
Position	Midfielder
Height	5'10"
Signed	July 1999
From	RC Lens (France)
Fee	£3.75m

Smicer, a £3.75m summer signing from Lens in France, has been impressed both with the ability and the spirit in the Liverpool camp since his move to Merseyside and he has no doubt that those two qualities will be more than enough to ensure the Liverpool fans will soon have plenty to shout about.

He says: 'I have come here to win trophies and I am certain that we have the players here to do that. Individually we have a good set of players with the likes of Robbie Fowler, Michael Owen, Jamie Redknapp and Patrik Berger, and collectively we have an excellent team who all get on well with each other. A good atmosphere within a squad is very important and I am delighted that we have that here.'

Smicer speaks from experience when he says that team morale can play a large part in the success of a club and he cites his time with Lens as a prime example. He says: 'In my last two years in France I helped Lens to win both the Championship and the League Cup. That was a great achievement for us and I am convinced it had a lot to do with the fact that all the players would work their socks off for each other.

'We finished thirteenth in the League in my first season in France and so nobody expected us to make such a massive improvement in the space of just two years. The atmosphere was brilliant, though, among the players and that was so crucial.

'It was the same when the Czech Republic reached the Final of the European Championship back in 1996. I don't think our side was stronger either technically or physically than the other teams, but we had that togetherness which enabled us to surprise the footballing world and reach the final against Germany.'

Smicer remains confident that Liverpool can surprise the rest of the Premiership this season and re-establish themselves as a footballing force in this country – and he is also hopeful that he can shake off his injury problems to play a major part in the club's challenge for honours.

He says: 'We have had a mixed season so far in as much as we have picked up a couple of brilliant results and then followed that up with some disappointing performances. It is never easy for a club to bed in some new players at the start of a season, but that problem has been even greater at Liverpool because so many new faces have arrived. It is still very early in the season and we still have a lot of time to make up the ground between ourselves and the leaders, but we have to start picking up results sooner rather than later.

'I am hoping from a personal point of view that the second half of the season will be better than the opening few months have been. I have had a few injuries already which has been very frustrating because I don't feel as though I have shown the Liverpool fans what I am capable of. I know that injuries are part and parcel of the game and we have to learn to accept them, but when you move to a new club you want to impress straight away and I haven't been able to do that.

'I have been very excited with what I have seen of English football so far, though. The game flows much more than it does in France where the referees are stopping the game for the most innocuous of challenges. There is a good rhythm to the game over here and it is wonderful to be a part of. Obviously the pace is very quick but good players will be able to adapt and I don't see any of us having a problem with the speed of the game once we have had time to adapt.'

Well on his way

Smicer may have struggled to make an instant impact on the field since his transfer to Anfield, but off it he has settled in without any problems thanks largely to the presence of a familiar face. He explains: 'I have been friends with Patrik Berger for many years and so from my point of view it is helpful to have him here because he speaks English and so can translate things for me. There are some French-speaking players at the club who I can speak with as well but the sooner I learn English the better.

'When I signed for Lens I didn't speak a word of French and so it was hard for me because I was always on my own. That hasn't been the case here which has ensured I have settled very quickly. I am just looking forward now to an injury-free run when I can finally show the Liverpool fans what I am capable of on the field.'

Smicer is a very exciting and talented midfielder.

Sander Westerveld
Serious Shot-Stopper

Goalkeeper Sander Westerveld looks ahead to what he hopes will be a long and fruitful Anfield career and admits: 'I don't want to look back on my footballing life in ten years' time with nothing to show for it'.

PLAYER STATS

Date of birth	October 23, 1974
Birthplace	Enschede (Holland)
Position	Goalkeeper
Height	6'4"
Signed	July 1999
From	Vitesse Arnhem (Holland)
Fee	£4m

Westerveld signed during the summer for a fee in excess of £4m – making him English football's most expensive-ever goalkeeper. But far from being daunted at the large transfer fee weighing on his shoulders, the Dutchman is intent on furthering his career with both club and country.

He says: 'People have asked me about the transfer fee and whether that is a problem, but it really isn't. I am the sort of person who likes to take the positive side from every situation and the fact that Liverpool were happy to pay so much money for me is great for my confidence.

'I never ever think about the transfer fee. Of course I know it is something people can throw at me if I play badly, but I am confident enough to believe that I will have more good games than bad ones for Liverpool and if I play to my potential then nobody can have any criticism of the money the club spent.'

Missed resource

Liverpool fans have been largely disappointed with the displays of their goalkeepers over recent years and so Westerveld could be forgiven for feeling under some pressure as Gérard Houllier's red revolution kicks into full force. But the Dutch number two keeper has always lived with pressure and expectation and considers his Anfield challenge as just another hurdle he has to overcome.

He says: 'I am lucky in many ways because so far in my career everything I have dreamed about has come true. Throughout my childhood I was very keen on becoming a footballer and so it was a great thrill for me when I turned professional at the age of 17.

'I then set myself the target of playing in the Dutch Premier League by the time I was 21 and I achieved that with Vitesse Arnhem. That was a great learning experience for me and gave me the chance to play top-level football week after week which is what I wanted.

'As a regular for my club I was keen to make the breakthrough on to the international stage and a few months back I won my first full cap in a friendly match for Holland against Brazil.

'The Dutch league is of a high standard but I always want to better myself and I fancied the prospect of a move to another country. England is a great place to play football and the Premiership is a terrific league. I am delighted to be here.'

Liverpool's new goalkeeper is a man who craves success, and if his past record is anything to go by then the Reds can look forward to a prosperous future.

He says: 'I am here now and I want to win things with Liverpool. I don't want the sort of career where I look back in ten years time and have nothing to show for it.

I believe in myself, in the other players and in the manager. Gérard Houllier said to me 'We want you' and that was all I needed to hear.'

Out of the blocks

Westerveld's early-season performances in the Liverpool goal have been encouraging. But such are the standards he has set for himself he considers any ball which flies into his goal to be a personal insult.

He says: 'I am a perfectionist in training and during matches. If I drop a ball in training then I am very angry with myself and it preys on my mind for a while. When a goal goes in that I know no other goalkeeper could have saved I do stop for a short time and reflect on what I might have done differently. I don't think that's a bad way for me to be because it keeps me concentrated and focused which is important.'

Adapting to the English style of play is never easy for newcomers to the Premiership and so training drills involving team-mates crashing into him as he comes to collect a cross have become part of Westerveld's daily routine at Melwood.

'It was necessary because the forwards challenge you a lot more than they do in Holland,' he explains. 'I always knew it would take time for me to fully adapt because Peter Schmeichel and Ed De Goey also needed time to get used to their new way of life.'

And although keeping balls out of the Liverpool net is his primary objective Westerveld is also keen to get into the scoring act at the other end of the field.

He says: 'I have always been able to kick the ball a long way and in the past I have come close on a couple of occasions to scoring a goal with a kick downfield. I am sure that somewhere someday I will surprise the opposition, maybe if the wind is behind me and I can get extra distance. It would be nice to score my first goal but so long as I keep as many clean sheets as possible through until the end of the season then I will be happy.'

Westerveld has already been noted as a hard-working, talented goalkeeper, who takes his football very seriously.

Stephane Henchoz
False Start

PLAYER STATS

Date of birth	September 7, 1974
Birthplace	Billens (Switzerland)
Position	Central Defender
Height	6'1"
Signed	July 1999
From	Blackburn Rovers
Fee	£3.5m

Liverpool defender Stephane Henchoz reflected on his early months at Anfield and admits: 'It has been one of the most frustrating times of my career'.

Henchoz had to wait patiently on the sidelines as his groin injury took longer than expected to heal and it wasn't until mid-September that he finally made his long-awaited Anfield debut.

'It was a terrible way to begin my Liverpool career,' says the Swiss star. 'I desperately wanted to start the season in the team at Sheffield Wednesday but it wasn't possible. I couldn't afford to take any chances with the injury because to do so could have been very costly and I didn't intend rushing back when there was a danger of the problem flaring up again.

'I am training properly now and so far I'm not feeling any effects from the injury at all. I hope that is all behind me now and I can concentrate on helping the Liverpool team over the course of the season.'

Henchoz signed from Blackburn Rovers in the summer following his former club's relegation from the Premiership simply because he didn't fancy life outside the top flight. He says: 'I had a great time at Blackburn and our relegation last season was very disappointing. I had to think about my career and when the chance came for me to sign for Liverpool I felt it was an offer I couldn't refuse. I am so impressed with all the players here because they are world-class and I have no doubts at all that this squad is capable of doing very well.'

Liverpool's defensive problems have once again been highlighted this season as several costly mistakes have led to important points being dropped but Henchoz is adamant that concentration is all that's needed for the Reds to shore up their back line.

He says: 'We have good defenders at Liverpool and so there is no reason why we can't be extremely tight at the back and make it very difficult for the opposition to score. That hasn't been happening this season, though, and so I can only assume that concentration is the key. We need to be on our toes for the 90 minutes because in the Premiership it only takes one sloppy moment for the opposition to punish you. It is a high-quality league and you have to be good both mentally and technically to succeed in it.

'Earlier in the season we conceded three goals against Manchester United at Anfield from crosses and that can't be allowed to happen. We need to deal with some situations better than we have been doing. People have to remember, though, that we are a new team and it will always take time for new players to adapt to their new club. We are on the right lines and at the moment that is the most important thing.'

While Henchoz had to wait many weeks for his Liverpool debut, he did play for Switzerland in a Euro 2000 qualifier against Belarus, much to the disgust of Anfield boss Gérard Houllier who has warned the Swiss FA that in future Henchoz will not be released for international duty when he isn't one hundred per cent fit.

Says Henchoz: 'All I want to do is play football. I love playing for my country and it gives me a great feeling to pull on the Swiss shirt, but it also fills me with pride now to wear the Liverpool shirt. They are one of the biggest clubs in the world and despite their lack of success over recent seasons they are still revered for what they have achieved over the years.

'I wouldn't have come to Liverpool if I didn't think they had the potential to be the best again because I am very ambitious and desperately want to win things.

'I am very pleased that the new players at the club have all done very well so far. I suppose I was different to the other new boys because I had Premiership experience from my Blackburn days whereas they had none. I don't think there is anything like this league throughout Europe in terms of excitement and the sheer pace of the game. The new lads have adapted brilliantly, though, which has been a big bonus.

'It was frustrating watching from the stands in the early part of the season because I really wanted to be out on the field helping out. I know what my strengths are and I know I can aid the defence but the crucial thing is that we defend as a team. We need eleven players working hard throughout the match if we are to be successful and from what I have seen from my time at the club so far we have a group of players who are desperate to be winners.'

Back after a long lay-off through injury, Stephane Henchoz (centre) is trying hard to provide strength in central defence for the Reds.

OLD GUARD

Patrik Berger
Back in the Frame

Rejuvenated midfield man Patrik Berger believes the improved discipline inside Anfield will be a crucial factor as the Reds go in search of success this season.

PLAYER STATS

Date of birth	November 10, 1973
Birthplace	Prague (Czech Republic)
Position	Midfielder
Height	6'1"
Signed	July 1996
From	Borussia Dortmund (Germany)
Fee	£3.5m

Berger has been an automatic selection in Gérard Houllier's teams since the Frenchman assumed total control of management affairs at Liverpool, and the Czech international has more than repaid that faith with some of the best performances of his Anfield career.

But with success at a premium over recent seasons Berger is desperate to win his first piece of silverware since joining the club and he firmly believes that the current managerial team are well on the way to shaping a Liverpool side good enough to challenge at the top of the table.

He says: 'There is no doubt about it that the atmosphere inside the club is better this season. There is a great spirit among the players and we all badly want to win for each other. Training is very enjoyable and we come into work of a morning looking forward to the day ahead. In any profession it is important to be happy and I am sure I speak for the rest of the lads when I say that we are all enjoying the challenge of being successful for Liverpool.

'I've certainly never been as happy since I signed for the club. I am playing week after week which is all I can ask for and it is up to me to produce consistent performances to stay there. I feel as though I am doing that and the manager obviously feels the same otherwise I

wouldn't be in the starting eleven.'

Blame-taker

It was the fact that Berger was so often made the scapegoat for defeats in the first year of his Liverpool career which led to him seriously considering a move away from Liverpool. Having signed after Euro '96, he made an instant impact at Anfield but was soon figuring less and less, much to his disappointment and frustration.

He admits: 'There have been some low times for me but hopefully they are all in the past now. When the new manager came in he told me I was going to be a big part of his plans and that is all I wanted to hear. It's never nice to watch from the sidelines when you feel you could do a job on the field but that is what was happening to me before the boss took over.

'It was a hard time for me because I am so happy in the city of Liverpool and my family are very settled. The bottom line, though, is that I am here for the football and not for the life, so when I wasn't playing I was very frustrated. Thankfully it has all worked out for me, but there were times when I honestly thought I would be leaving the club.'

Berger's trickery and speed in midfield combined with a priceless ability to score goals have made him a hero with the Liverpool fans who will always support a player they feel is giving his all for the club.

'That is definitely the case with me,' he says. 'Every time I go on to the field I am desperate to play well and produce my best form. It doesn't happen all the time but I am pleased that there is a consistency in my game.

'It is important we play consistently as a team because that has been our undoing over recent seasons. We know what the problem has been but we haven't been able to sort it out. Hopefully the new training methods and the new ideas the manager has brought into the club will reap rewards as the season goes on.'

Tried and tested

Berger is now one of the more experienced members of the Liverpool team having figured in over 100 games for the club. He knows what it is like to try to settle into a new country and that is why he has been doing his best to help out the current crop of Liverpool newcomers whenever possible.

'The new players who have joined the club are all high in quality and that is the important thing. If they are happy on the field then they will settle into their new life very quickly, as I discovered. Vladimir Smicer is a player I have known for a long time and I have no doubts he will be a quality addition to the squad. He is great on the ball going forward and he will work very hard for the team which is what you need from flair players to go with their natural skill.

'If we keep our squad largely free from injury as the season goes on then I am sure we will have a great chance of being successful. It is too early to say whether or not this will be our year, but I am sure that we have enough quality to at least win something. That has to be our aim.'

Berger was brought to Liverpool for his skill and pace. Here he shows Patrick Vieira a clean pair of heels.

Robbie Fowler
A Fresh Start

PLAYER STATS	
Date of birth	April 9, 1975
Birthplace	Liverpool
Position	Striker
Height	5'11"
Signed	Trainee

Vice-captain Robbie Fowler is hell-bent on ensuring he makes the headlines for the right reasons this season.

His highly publicised – and costly – misdemeanours last season have now been consigned to the dustbin of history as far as he is concerned and all he is looking forward to is the chance to show the world the new, more mature Robbie Fowler who remains one of the deadliest strikers in Europe.

He says: 'I have apologised for what happened last season and at the end of the day you can only say sorry so many times. As far as I am concerned that is all behind me now. Of course I will learn from my mistakes and I won't be repeating them but I want my performances on the pitch to be making the headlines from now on.'

Fowler faced a six-match suspension at the end of last season for two well-documented incidents, but boss Gérard Houllier backed him all the way and surprised many when he appointed Fowler the club's vice-captain.

Says Fowler: 'The boss has done brilliantly for me and he backed me through the bad times which meant a great deal. I honestly did think it might be better for me to leave Liverpool because everything I did was being analysed, but the manager sat me down and took away all the fears I had. In my heart I never wanted to leave but I thought the time was coming when I would have no other option.

'I am delighted to still be here, though, and I intend to be around for many years to come. I really believe the manager is on the verge of something big here because he has brought in so many good players who have improved the quality of our squad and when we click together on a consistent basis we will be a very difficult team to beat.'

Fowler kicked off the season with a goal on the opening day at Sheffield Wednesday and also scored a stunning goal against Arsenal at Anfield in what many believe was his best performance in a Liverpool shirt for a long time. He says: 'I have made a decent start to the season but there is still more to come from me yet. We have had some good results, but also some disappointing ones as well which again has highlighted our problem of inconsistency. The wins against Leeds and Arsenal were brilliant for us in terms of confidence, especially after a couple of bad defeats.

Robbie Fowler has been a changed man this season. Luckily, his goalscoring prowess has remained the same, as he demonstrated here with this goal against Arsenal.

'To go to a place like Leeds and win was excellent. I didn't play at all well on the night but fortunately the rest of the lads were great and we picked up a good three points. Then against Arsenal we were magnificent for the whole 90 minutes and fully deserved the victory. I don't know why I always seem to score against Arsenal. All strikers have teams they have great success against and I have always done well against them, which is strange considering how good their defence has been for so many years.

'Even though we have had some good results I don't think the critics will ever totally get off our backs. We know we are a good team and hopefully everyone else

knows that as well, but with the success this club has had over the years we have incredible standards to live up to.

'That pressure will always be there but I am sure we can cope with it.'

In for England

As Fowler goes in search of more Premiership goals this season he is also desperate to make the permanent step up into the England team. For a player of his talent to have little more than ten full caps to his name is a poor return, but he is hoping that international selection will soon become the norm.

He says: 'I love playing for England. Any player will say they would love to play for their country and I am no different. If I am

being honest then I have to say that I should have earned more caps, but time is still on my side and I have plenty of years ahead of me to get more international recognition. I haven't scored as many goals as I would have liked for England but I retain complete confidence in my ability to score at the highest level.'

Liverpool fans are more concerned that Fowler continues his prolific club scoring form this season as the Reds go in search of honours. He says: 'The Premiership is a very good league with a lot of quality sides. We know we can compete with them all on our day, and once we learn to consistently grind out results when we're not playing well then we will be on the way to achieving some success.'

Steven Gerrard
Another Rising Star

Youngster Steven Gerrard has already achieved his pre-season ambitions and now has his sights set much higher.

PLAYER STATS

Date of birth	May 30, 1980
Birthplace	Liverpool
Position	Midfielder
Height	6'1"
Signed	Trainee

The Liverpool midfield man began the season in the hope that he would at least sample some first-team football and also experience his first taste of international action with the under-21s.

Several months on, Gerrard has been an integral part of the Anfield engine-room and has even earned a man of the match award while representing his country. Needless to say, the 19-year-old local lad describes the start to his season as 'a dream come true.'

He says: 'Last season I was given the chance to show people what I was capable of and I think I did quite well. Over the summer I was happy with the way things were going for me and I was looking forward to the new season, even though I knew we had signed a lot of new players and so my chances of playing in the first team were likely to be remote.

'We had a few injuries early in the season, though, which opened the door for me. The manager was obviously impressed with what I did last year because he gave me a place in the middle of the field and told me to carry on playing the way I had been. I think the fans had high expectations of me as well and I was very keen to prove that I wasn't a flash in the pan and that I could perform over a long period of time.'

Another's misfortune

It was the unfortunate injury to German midfielder Dietmar Hamann which gave Gerrard his chance and this season he has already shown why England under-21 boss Howard Wilkinson regards him as one of the brightest talents in the Premiership.

'A lot of people have been saying a lot of nice things about me,' says Gerrard. 'Of course that is pleasing from my point of view but I know the importance of maintaining my standards. I have proved I can play for Liverpool in the Premiership without looking out of place and that means a lot to me but I still have a lot to learn in the game.

'Being called up for England was another great honour for me and it is great from my point of view that I now have some international experience to go alongside the experience I have picked up in club football. I played against both Luxembourg and Poland in the under-21 matches and I think things went quite well for me. We had already qualified at the top of our group and so there was no great pressure to win the matches, but we did beat Luxembourg easily before losing out to Poland which was disappointing.

'Against Luxembourg I scored the first goal and even got the man of the match award after the game which was a very nice surprise. It is important for me now that I stay involved with the Liverpool squad to ensure I carry on being selected for the under-21s with England. Like every footballer it is my dream to play for England.'

National coach Kevin Keegan has already invited Gerrard down to the England training camp prior to an international friendly earlier in the year, which perhaps offers the Liverpool youngster an insight into Keegan's thoughts on him as a player.

'That was a tremendous couple of days for me with the England party and it gave me some sort of idea of what is involved. I was very nervous in the first practice match because I didn't want to give the ball away and look stupid so I just concentrated on doing the simple thing and gaining confidence along the way. Hopefully that won't be the last time with the full squad because I really enjoyed myself.'

When Liverpool boss Gérard Houllier has all of his multi-million pound players available and free of injury Gerrard appreciates that he may not be included in the starting eleven, but he is currently happy in the knowledge that he has proved he can be relied upon to perform well in the Premiership when necessary.

He says: 'It would obviously be great if I stayed in the team right through until the end of the season but I would be being extremely optimistic if I thought that was going to happen. The squad is full of world-class international players and I understand the manager may leave me out when they are all fit. But I will be working harder than ever in training to try and keep my place in the side.

'At the start of the season I wanted to play at least 15 games for Liverpool and also to play for England. Now I am setting my targets higher and I want to play as many games as possible for both club and country.'

Steven Gerrard has won critical acclaim for his performances in a Liverpool shirt.

Michael Owen

Scoring is his Business — and Business is Good

Super striker Michael Owen finally returned to fitness after an agonising five months on the sidelines admitting: 'It was only a matter of time before I suffered a low point in my footballing career'.

Owen's hamstring injury sidelined him for the latter stages of last season as well as the opening matches of the current campaign, and with important matches for England sandwiched in between it is clear to see why the young striker has been a frustrated figure as his injury took longer to heal than first expected.

But now he is back, scoring goals, and he is desperate to make up for lost time. He says: 'It has been an extremely frustrating time for me but I have tried to remain positive. It was always going to be just a matter of time before I was fit again, but the weeks dragged on without too much improvement being made and that was hard to take.

'Thankfully we got there in the end, though, and now I am feeling as fit and as strong as ever. It is horrible watching from the sidelines when all you want to do is be on the field playing, especially at the start of the season when there is so much optimism around the place.'

Much-needed rest

Despite being confined to the treatment room for the best part of the last five months, in hindsight Owen believes his injury may have been a blessing in disguise.

He explains: 'I obviously wasn't thinking that way at the time, but if I am being honest then maybe I will benefit from the rest. I am still only young and I have played a lot of games over the last three years. Maybe the injury was my body's way of telling me to slow down and take a rest. It is impossible to keep on going without taking a break and so now I am hoping the rest will have done me some good.

'It goes without saying that I was concerned that the injury wasn't healing as quickly as we would have liked, but I just had to remain patient and not try to rush things. Strikers like myself rely on their pace and so it was very important I didn't rush back before I was ready otherwise it is likely the hamstring would have been damaged again and I could easily have been back to square one. I have been guided by the medical staff at Liverpool and have worked very hard myself to regain fitness.

'I went to Germany to see a specialist and the advice he offered me seems to have worked. He gave me a set of exercises and massages which helped loosen my back which then allowed more blood to flow into my legs. If I continue with these exercises for the rest of my career then I am hopeful the injury won't flare up again.'

That thought will be shared by the Liverpool staff and fans alike: the fitness of

Michael Owen is crucial to the club's chance of success this season.

He says: 'At least the summer break ensured I didn't actually miss too many games and so that is some consolation. It goes without saying that during my first few games back in the team I was a bit worried about whether I would suffer any reaction from the injury but that never happened. I've had no pain from the hamstring at all and haven't been restricted in any way which is exactly what I was looking for.

'I want to steer clear of injuries now and play as many games as I can between now and the end of the season. I have had a good break and am ready to go again. We have made a decent start to the season and the lads have picked up some good results already. If we can maintain the form we have shown in patches then we could do well this year, but the Premiership is a hard league and we need to maintain some form of consistency.'

Owen's return to club football is great news for the country as well, with many fans believing the time is right for Liverpool's young striker to become an automatic selection for his country.

'That's a decision for the England manager to make,' says Owen. 'I am always pleased to be playing for my country and I think I have proved that I can score goals at international level. If I keep on doing the business for Liverpool then hopefully more England caps will come my way.'

Owen is hoping his enforced rest from the game at the start of the season will pay dividends in the long run.

Jamie Redknapp
The New Captain

PLAYER STATS

Date of birth	June 25, 1973
Birthplace	Barton-on-Sea
Position	Midfielder
Height	6′
Signed	1991
From	Bournemouth
Fee	£350,000

Anfield skipper Jamie Redknapp is a man on a mission this season.

Having described his appointment as club captain as 'one of the happiest days of my life', the 26-year-old midfielder intends to help the Reds rid themselves of the unwanted 'underachievement' label and in the process help the club reach the top of the English game once again.

Redknapp was the obvious choice to succeed Paul Ince when manager Gérard Houllier made it clear Ince had no part to play in his future Anfield plans and he now wants to follow in the footsteps of Liverpool captains of the past who have been able to celebrate lifting the most prized possessions in European football.

'I look at the players I am following and it is a great honour,' he admits. 'The likes of Phil Thompson, Graeme Souness and John Barnes have all been great captains at Liverpool and I would love to achieve some of the success they all had.

'When the manager asked me to be the captain I was taken aback. It was a great moment for me and it took me all of about two seconds to tell him I would be delighted to accept the offer. It means the world to me to captain Liverpool. I was made skipper a couple of times last season when Incey was injured and that was a great privilege, but to have the armband on a full-time basis is incredible.

'I am sure I can be the sort of leader everyone wants me to be on the field. I may not be the sort of player to go around screaming and shouting, but I will make sure everybody is doing what they are supposed to be because at the end of the day we are all aiming for the same thing and that is success.'

Could do better

Unfortunately success has been in short supply over recent seasons at Anfield and, at his age, Redknapp admits that his career to date should probably have been rewarded with more silverware than has been the case so far.

He says: 'I am 26 now and an international player. I know I should have won more than I have in the game but everybody at Liverpool would say exactly the same thing. We are more disappointed than anybody that we haven't been successful but there is still time for that to change.

'We have a new squad of players here now who have all done really well and hopefully they can help us to take that extra step. We have been close to some success over recent years but in the end we just haven't been good enough to keep a consistent run of results going.

'The changes that were made over the summer needed to be made, in my opinion. Of course it is always going to be a gamble when so many new faces arrive at the same time but as soon as we mixed with the new lads it was clear to see that they were good players as well as being good people. The important thing is that they all

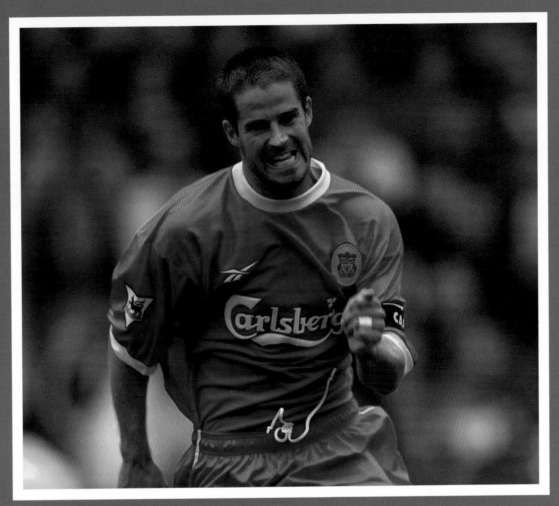

Jamie Redknapp is one of the game's great passers – he scores some pretty good goals too!

wanted to come to Liverpool and they are all determined to achieve success as well. We have a lot of talent in the squad right now and it would be a shame if we didn't realise our potential.'

Redknapp was the subject of some transfer speculation during the summer months which led to manager Gérard Houllier taking the unusual step of making a club statement insisting his new captain was not for sale.

Says Redknapp: 'Since I have been at Liverpool there always seems to have been some speculation linking me with a move away. Usually it is one of the

southern clubs reported to be interested in me and I think the journalists look at that, see that I am from the South and so assume that I must be unhappy here and am looking for a move away.

'Nothing could be further from the truth. I have been at Liverpool for a long time now and I love everything about the place. The coaching staff are first-class and, as I have said, we have a bunch of players who are the equal of any other squad in the country. We know that, but we have to prove it on the field on a consistent basis.

'I am very happy in Liverpool and I love the city. The fans have always been

tremendous to me and I am very settled in the area. I have no interest whatsoever in a move away because I feel I can achieve what I want to with Liverpool.

'We are not hiding the fact that this is a very big season for us. We at least need to show that we have improved from last season which was extremely disappointing for us all. I know there is extra responsibility on me now that I am the captain and I am sure I will thrive on the new challenge. I'm not a baby in this team any more and I realise I will have to lead by example if we are going to have a good season.'

David Thompson
Seizing the Day

PLAYER STATS	
Date of birth	September 12, 1977
Birthplace	Birkenhead
Position	Midfield
Height	5'7"
Signed	Trainee

Midfield man David Thompson believes he has finally earned the trust of manager Gérard Houllier – but he admits it may not be enough to guarantee him a first team place at Anfield.

Having spent much of his career excelling in the reserves but struggling to make the breakthrough into the first-team, Thompson could have been forgiven for becoming increasingly frustrated with his lack of Premiership opportunities.

But that frustration has undoubtedly turned to delight this season as Thompson has been given the chance to impress in midfield following a spate of injuries to key first-team regulars.

Says Thompson: 'I always knew it was going to need a few injuries for me to get my chance but I have played in a lot of the games this season and I am very pleased with the way things have gone for me. In my position I knew if I didn't take the

chance then it could be a while before another one came along and so I was determined to give it everything I had.

'As a result I think the manager has a lot more faith in me now than perhaps he did beforehand. I have proved to him that I can play in the Premiership and that I can do a job for Liverpool. I'm not sure he always thought that, so it is nice from my point of view that I have persuaded him otherwise.

'I'm not getting carried away, though, because we have a big squad of players here and when everyone is fit it remains to be seen whether I will stay in the team. For now I am just pleased that I have proved myself because I would have hated the months to go by without any chance in the

first team coming my way.'

Thompson's drive and enthusiasm combined with his undoubted skill in midfield has made him a favourite among Liverpool fans, and the under-21 England man realises it is time for the players to repay the fans for the way they have stuck with the club during recent lean years.

He says: 'The supporters have been really brilliant and all the players appreciate the way they have got right behind us, even when results haven't been going our way. We understand their frustrations because the players want success every bit as much as the fans but we realise it is our duty to go out and win something for them.

'We usually do quite well in the big matches, although defeats against Manchester United and Everton already this season have been hard to take, but against the smaller clubs we struggle. That has been the case for some years now and it has cost us dearly. Last season apart, we had been in the top four for a few years running and our bad results against teams we should have beaten probably cost us the title.

'We have to be more professional and also more clinical. There have been times when we have been in a comfortable position in games but then we haven't tried to kill the match off. Instead we have become a bit sloppy and ended up conceding an equalising goal. Good teams and title-winning teams can grind out results and that is something we need to learn to do.'

England expects

Thompson's form this season in a revamped Liverpool midfield has seen him called into the under-21 squad for recent matches with Luxembourg and Poland. While gratefully accepting any international recognition which comes his way, the Liverpool-born youngster wants to concentrate his effort first and foremost on his club career.

He says: 'Being called up for the England matches was a great honour. It wasn't an entirely new experience for me because I have been selected before, but it is nice to see that the international coaches are aware of me and of what I can do. I would love to stay involved with the England set-up but the most important thing for me is to carry on playing well for Liverpool.

'I have been at the club for many years now and in the past I have wondered whether I would ever make the breakthrough. I even went on loan to Swindon a few years back to get some first-team experience under my belt. I am much more confident now that I can stake a regular claim for myself in the team. I am under no illusions that it is going to be very difficult because the manager has signed a lot of new players and so competition for a place in the starting eleven has increased, but I have proved that I can perform in the Premiership and now it is up to the gaffer whether he sticks with me.'

Thompson has pleaded his case on the pitch for inclusion in the first team.

LIFE IN LIVERPOOL –

SANDER WESTERVELD

Dutch goalkeeper Sander Westerveld admits he was more than a little wary before his first visit to Liverpool following reports that he was moving to a poor city. But his experience of Liverpool and its people so far has convinced him that he should never have listened to the scare stories as he embarks on his Premiership mission at Anfield.

'I absolutely love the place,' he says. 'When I told people back home in Holland that I was moving to Liverpool some of them told me it wasn't a nice place to live and that the city was not too well off. I can't believe how wrong they were because I fell in love with everything about the place as soon as I first saw it. I think people in Europe have a bad image of Liverpool for some reason and it is a pity they can't come over and see it for themselves because they would return home wondering how they could have been so wrong.

'Liverpool is a major city and it has everything in it that you would want. The shopping malls are excellent and there are lots of nice restaurants around to choose from when you are eating out. I honestly don't have anything bad to say about Liverpool and I am surprised that there are people who do. I understand they went through a bad time some years back but there isn't much evidence of that around today. I know there has been a lot of rebuilding work carried out and a lot of investment has been made but from what I have seen the place is lively and vibrant and is certainly a very nice city in which to live.'

As well as being impressed with what Liverpool has to offer as a city Westerveld, signed from Dutch outfit Vitesse Arnhem in the summer to replace David James in the Anfield goal, has already struck up an immediate rapport with the people.

He says: 'Liverpool people are really nice and very, very helpful. It could have been difficult for me moving to a new country if

RIGHT, LEFT AND BELOW:
Famous views of St John's
Beacon, a Ferry Cross the
Mersey and the Liverpool
Anglican Cathedral.

St John's Beacon towering above the Liverpool skyline.

the people weren't very welcoming but that hasn't been the case here at all. I recently read an interview with the Rangers striker Michael Mols and he was saying that the biggest problem foreign players have when they move to a new country is having to adjust to their new environment. I could see how that would be the case for some players but I have felt at home since Day One in Liverpool.

'One big difference between the fans here and in Holland is the respect they show you. When you are walking down the street in Holland it is often the case that they will shout at you behind your back which of course isn't very nice, even if they are shouting something positive. It is totally different here, though. They want to come up to you, shake your hand and say 'Good Luck' which I find to be very refreshing.

'When I have been in restaurants with my girlfriend in Liverpool it has been very noticeable that supporters will wait until you have finished your meal and paid the bill before they try to ask for an autograph. And they will always begin the conversation by saying 'Excuse me' or 'Sorry to bother you' first which is really nice. Of course there is never any problem and I am always willing to sign autographs and pose for pictures with the fans. I just think they show you so much respect and that means a great deal to me because I have a lot of respect for them as well.'

Added bonus

Westerveld took a look around Liverpool before agreeing to put pen to paper on his Anfield contract but he admits that football was always going to be the number one reason for moving to England.

He says: 'Obviously it's better if you have a nice place to live but at the end of the day I came here for the football. It is a great bonus for me that the city is so nice as well because now I have the best of both worlds and I couldn't be happier.

'My girlfriend has moved over with me and she is currently studying at university so it is good that she has also settled in well. It could have been difficult if she didn't like Liverpool because it is important to me that she is happy as well. We are both very content here and of course we are extremely thankful to the fans who have helped us settle in quicker than we might have imagined we would.'

Westerveld is also more than happy with his new team-mates who have quickly welcomed him into the Anfield fold. He says: 'The players at Liverpool are all great people and everybody is so friendly. We had a lot of new faces arriving for pre-season training in the summer and it is to the credit of those lads who have been here for a long time that they went out of their way to make us all feel welcome. After a short time it didn't feel like we were newcomers to the club at all. Everybody works hard for each other and nothing is too much trouble. The manager and his staff quite rightly put a big emphasis on teamwork and team spirit and that is something we have in abundance throughout the squad.

'Training is always enjoyable and I always wake up looking forward to the day ahead. We have a good laugh but we also do a lot of serious work as we prepare for the game at the weekend. I have training sessions with our goalkeeping coach Joe Corrigan and he has been a great help to me during my early days at the club. I am sure I will improve as a goalkeeper during my time at Liverpool and at the age of 24 I know my best days are still ahead of me.'

MICHAEL OWEN

Striking star Michael Owen has the kind of lifestyle the majority of people can only dream about – but there is a big price to pay for his elevation to superstar status.

Liverpool's reputation for its maritime history is high all over the world.

Away from football, one of Michael's passions is golf. Not suprisingly, he is a pretty good player.

The Liverpool and England man continues to show maturity way beyond his 19 years as he comes to terms with the fact that he is now a household name and a role model for thousands of football-mad children from all over the world.

'It goes without saying that my life has changed a lot in the last two years,' admits Owen. 'There has been so much publicity and so much attention that I suppose it was bound to be the case that people would want to talk to me all the time and ask for autographs and pictures. I suppose it means I am doing well if I am always in the papers, but to be honest at first it did come as a bit of a shock to me.'

Owen's form for Liverpool during his early years in the Premiership catapulted him to fame amongst Reds fans, but it was his exploits for England – and in particular THAT goal against Argentina – which opened the door for him on a world stage.

He says: 'People often ask me about the goal against Argentina and I have to admit it did a lot for me. After that goal fans from all over the world knew about me and the interest in my career went absolutely crazy for a time. I had cameramen following me everywhere and journalists even wanted to talk to my family and my girlfriend which was sometimes difficult for them to cope with.

'I have seen the goal many times on video and I never get tired of watching it. I hope I can score more goals like that one in the future, though I doubt that would be possible.

'I had lots and lots of requests for interviews and commercial offers poured in from everywhere after the World Cup, but I was determined not to let anything get in the way of my football which was always going to be the most important thing. I was a level-headed lad before breaking into the Liverpool team and I like to think I have remained that way since.

'I had good people around me who looked after the commercial side of things and I only accepted a couple of the offers that came my way because I felt that to take on any more would be to the detriment of my game.'

Owen has always lived away from the hustle and bustle of Liverpool city centre, admitting he prefers the quieter life. He says: 'I am very happy with the way things are going at the moment and I couldn't have wished for any more. I still live in the area which I grew

The Liver Building – one of Liverpool's most famous landmarks.

up in and I feel comfortable there which is important to me. Obviously it is hard for me to go out socially because I would be recognised which is very nice because people are great towards me, but at the same time I do need time away from that side of the job.

'I can't do the sort of things other lads my age do, but at the same time I wouldn't swap my lifestyle for anything. I am playing for one of the biggest clubs in Europe and at the moment everything about my life is great.

'I get hundreds of letters from supporters every week asking for autographs and I always try to send a reply because I think it is important to appreciate the fans. They have been brilliant towards me since I broke into the Liverpool team and if they want an autograph then I am always willing to send them one.'

Take the pressure

Some young men of Owen's age might have buckled under the sort of intense media interest he has generated, but he has received praise from all quarters for the way he has come to terms with the undoubted changes in his life.

He says: 'I think I have coped quite well. To be honest it has never bothered me when microphones have been placed under my mouth and journalists have been asking all kinds of questions. I try to answer them as honestly as I can and I certainly have never felt intimidated or anything. There was a time when I was on the back pages of the newspapers virtually every day and the lads at Liverpool gave me a lot of stick about it, but thankfully most of the things written about me so far have been complimentary.

'I'm not naïve enough to think that will always be the case, though. I am not

letting any of the publicity go to my head simply because I am sure there will be a time in my career when I don't do so well and as a result the people who have been praising me so far will try to knock me down. I am mentally tough enough to cope with that whenever the time comes.'

It is a credit to Owen's professionalism that his stunning form has been maintained even when the eyes of the footballing world have been on his performances. 'I always want to do well,' he says. 'I go on to the field before every

match believing I am going to score because as a striker you need to have that confidence in your own ability.

'Defenders know a lot more about me now and so mark me tighter but it is up to me to develop my game and work out new ways of escaping their attentions. I have scored goals all through my junior career and have continued in that vein for the Liverpool first team. I intend to score many more during the rest of my career.'

Clearly the Michael Owen bandwagon has a long way to roll just yet!

Aware of the value of the coaching he received as a boy, Michael is keen to play his part. Here he trains some children at the Anfield County Junior School.

TRAINING
AT MELWOOD

Gérard Houllier in pensive mood as he watches training at Melwood.

All of Liverpool's greatest triumphs in their illustrious history may have been achieved on the football field – but all the planning for their many successes took place two miles away from Anfield.

Melwood has been the club's training headquarters for many years and it is there where some of the best footballers the game has ever seen have learned and developed their trade.

Befitting a club the size and stature of Liverpool, Melwood is a state-of-the-art training complex with every facility required to help the stars of today repeat the success story achieved by the heroes of yesterday.

The players are put through their paces with strenuous training sessions in the early part of the week, but as match day on the Saturday approaches, the intensity of the sessions lessens and tactical preparations take over.

Manager Gérard Houllier is surrounded by a set of quality coaches who aid him on the training field, and often he even leaves them to look after sessions while he ploughs through the mound of paperwork building in his office.

'We have a very good set of coaches and an excellent set of players,' says assistant boss Phil Thompson. 'Training is serious but enjoyable where the players work extremely hard but also have some fun along the way. It is important to make sure the players enjoy their training because otherwise you wouldn't get the best out of them and that would be to the detriment of their game.'

TOP: Patrik Berger.

BELOW: Danny Murphy.

Early start

Training times differ during the week but usually the players are required to be at Melwood by 10am for a 10.30 start. The only breakfast permitted before training is a high-energy cereal bar but the players are able to eat a full lunch once the session has come to an end.

Regular meetings between Gérard Houllier and his staff – Phil Thompson, Sammy Lee, Patrice Bergues and Joe Corrigan – take place first thing in the morning when the training session for the day is planned.

It is Sammy Lee who usually begins putting the players through their paces with a series of stretching exercises designed to loosen muscles before any running or ball work takes place. Liverpool have always placed a great deal of pride on their passing football and therefore it is no surprise that small-sided games regularly take place at Melwood, with the emphasis on ball control and accuracy of passing.

Gérard Houllier often calls training to a sudden stop if he wishes to make an observation about something he has seen, while from the sidelines the other coaches are almost always shouting words of instruction or encouragement to the players.

It may surprise some to discover that training on a normal day at Melwood lasts less than two hours, before the players can retire to the changing rooms to shower and then to the canteen for something to eat.

Different for 'keepers

As the outfield players train on one of the many pitches at Melwood, the goalkeepers disappear into the far corner of the complex to be put through their paces by the club's goalkeeping coach Joe Corrigan.

'I would have loved the chance to have a

TOP: Sammy Lee.
ABOVE: Phil Thompson.

TOP: Phil Thompson.
ABOVE: Patrice Bergues.

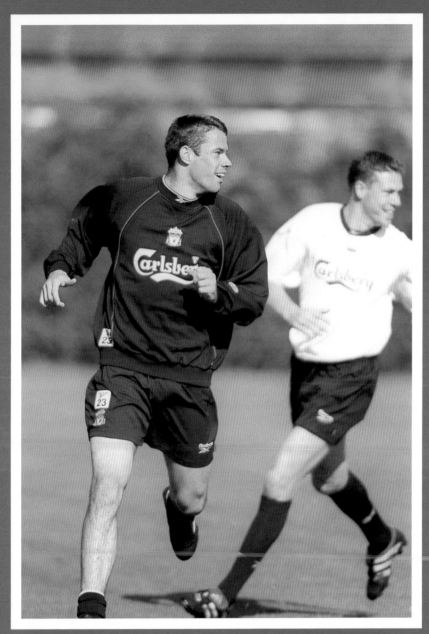

Jamie Carragher and Erik Meijer during a practice game.

 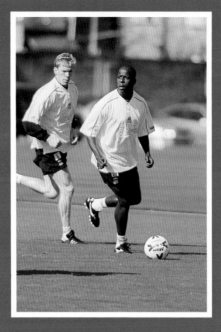 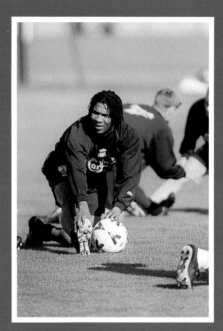

LEFT TO RIGHT: Phil Babb, Steve Staunton, Titi Camara and Rigobert Song are put through their paces.

goalkeeping coach when I was playing,' admits Joe. 'It is a specialised position on the field and so it is only right that the goalkeepers are given different training routines than the other players.

'I try to make the sessions enjoyable but I have to say that the goalkeepers all work extremely hard and they set themselves very high standards. Sometimes they undergo a punishing training schedule which takes a lot out of them but they realise they are the ones who will benefit on a Saturday afternoon. We have had a number of goalkeepers here over recent years and some of them have been foreigners which is a different challenge for me because foreign 'keepers sometimes do things differently compared to English ones.

I enjoy trying to get the best out of our 'keepers, though, and I have no doubts that they are all good enough to make good careers for themselves in the game.'

A small sprinkling of Liverpool supporters often watch from the sidelines as the players work hard at their game at Melwood, while other fans instead opt to climb one of the walls surrounding the complex and view training from a less comfortable position.

The players by and large enjoy the sessions and without exception they all realise the importance of taking training seriously every day. Midfielder Patrik Berger says: 'The discipline in our training these days is very good. We do a lot of stamina work but the emphasis is always

on the ball work and I am pleased that we have inventive training sessions where we have a lot of fun.'

Homework

Captain Jamie Redknapp often stays behind at the end of training to concentrate on his free kicks or passing ability. From all areas of the field he fires the ball into the corner of the net and he admits his dedication is in the pursuit of perfection. 'I always want to better myself as a player and that is why I sometimes stay behind after training and work on my game. I am always willing to listen and learn and the coaching staff here are people who have great experience in football, and so I would be a fool not to listen to their advice.'

RIGHT: Vegard Heggem is interviewed by a European television station.

BELOW: Michael Owen finds training a good laugh as well as hard work.

Striker Michael Owen is equally enthusiastic about his desire to become an even better goalscorer. He says: 'I missed pre-season training this year and that was a big disadvantage to me because it meant I was lagging behind the rest of the lads. I don't think anybody actually likes the pre-season work because it takes some time to get your fitness towards the standard it should be but the importance of a good month's work before the season starts cannot be under-estimated.

'I do enjoy training when the season starts and it is important for me to score goals at Melwood because it keeps me sharp for when the match comes along on a Saturday afternoon.'

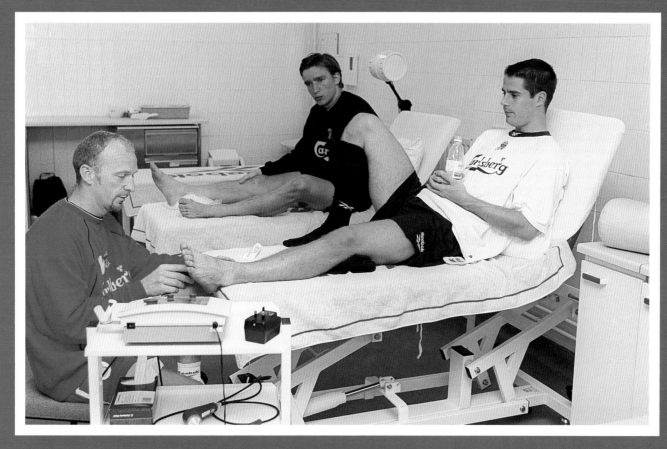

Vladimir Smicer and Jamie Redknapp receive attention in the treatment room from physio Mark Browes.

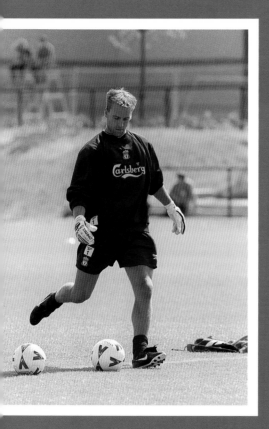

Westerveld takes everything seriously.

Once the players have finished their training session they will often go to the gym to do some work on strengthening both the upper and lower body. The gym at Melwood is one of the most advanced in Europe, and its state-of-the-art equipment is capable of analysing the performances of every player on a particular piece of equipment and then printing out the results to enable the medical and coaching staff to keep abreast of the progress of a particular player.

Extra treatment

Liverpool also employ a full-time masseur, Garry Armer, to treat the players as and when necessary at the training ground. Says Garry: 'After physical activity it is normal for people to feel a stiffness in their muscles and that painful feeling can be removed through massage. Massage helps to increase the blood flow to the muscles which pushes out the lactic acid that causes the pain.

'Some players enjoy having a massage and some don't. It is entirely up to the individual but I think more and more players now are becoming aware as to the benefits it can provide. The morning after every first-team game the players report to Melwood for a warm-down and that is when most of them generally want to have a massage. It can last anything up to 40 minutes, depending on the player, and I can see up to 15 players a day. There used to be a stigma attached to the idea of massage but that isn't the case any more and the players at Liverpool are certainly comfortable with it.'

Unless there is training in the afternoon

as well – as is sometimes the case in the earlier part of the week – the players are free to leave for home once they have had some lunch in the Melwood canteen. It is often said that one of the perks of being a footballer is the amount of free time you are granted to spend at your leisure, and the players appreciate the importance of relaxing as much as possible in between training sessions.

Young midfielder Steven Gerrard says: 'I play a lot of golf when I am not training because that is very relaxing; otherwise I sit at home and get my feet up as much as possible. As the week goes on it is important to rest as much as you can because a Premiership match really does test you physically and if you aren't right then you will let yourself and the rest of the team down.'

Rigobert Song with his feet on the ball…

… Berger and Heggem with their heads on the ball.

LEFT: Robbie Fowler is always ready to shoot for goal.
RIGHT: The players even have to jump through hoops.
BELOW: Owen, Carragher, Fowler and Staunton have a good time…

THE
ACADEMY

Liverpool manager Gérard Houllier may well have spent upwards of £25m bringing new foreign talent to Anfield over the past few months, but the club's most important investment of recent years lies a few miles away from Anfield, in Kirkby.

At a cost of £12m, Liverpool's acclaimed Soccer Academy stands alone as the best in Britain and gives the club's stars of the future the best possible chance of realising their footballing dreams. The Academy has ten grass pitches, three of which are floodlit. There is also a synthetic pitch – regarded as the best of its kind in the country – with its own floodlighting and spectator accommodation.

An Operations Centre was built which houses the dressing rooms and a state-of-the-art physiotherapy and medical centre. Administration offices, dining facilities and classrooms for youngsters are also situated in the Operations Centre. More recently the building of an indoor sports hall has been completed which allows training indoors during inclement weather.

Before the Academy was built all of Liverpool's first team and youth team players trained at Melwood, but the construction of the Academy now ensures that Steve Heighway, Academy Director, and his team have an even better chance of continuing their remarkable record of transforming talented youngsters into first-team stars.

Says Steve: 'It was becoming clear that Melwood wasn't big enough to cater for everybody who wanted to use it and so we had to do some serious thinking. The idea for the Academy was first discussed four years ago. As with any club the team comes first but we needed to think of ourselves and it made sense to try to relocate somewhere else.

'The first team is about winning games on a Saturday, whereas we are about preparing players for the future and monitoring their development. The two sides of the club are completely different and so we had to make a decision.

'We had wonderful support from the Chairman and the Board of Directors. They have made a considerable investment in the Academy and have always offered us their one hundred per cent backing. It cost a lot of money to build but we are convinced it was money well spent.

'I have to admit that the finished product is better than even I imagined it would be. The Academy is a fantastic place to work and it is a great privilege for all of us to be involved. Youngsters at Liverpool today have a great chance of being successful because they have good people around them as well as the best possible surroundings in which to learn about the game.'

Good examples

Before the final seal of approval was given to the design of the Academy, the Liverpool staff took the opportunity to see what other European clubs were doing.

Says Steve: 'There are a number of clubs from the continent who have an excellent record as far as youth football and youth development is concerned and so it was important we took the time out to visit those places. We visited Auxerre in France and Ajax in Holland where we picked up some very useful ideas.

'Together with our own thoughts and ideas I think we have done the best possible job.'

With phases one and two of the Academy project already complete there remains just the one addition to be made – the construction of a 30-bed residential lodge to provide accommodation for youngsters from the UK, Ireland and further afield.

'It will be a magnificent addition to the complex when it is completed,' says Steve. 'To be able to offer boys accommodation while they are with us is an excellent attraction and it should give us a greater chance of continuing to bring the best youngsters to Liverpool.

'All the staff are fully aware of the massive responsibility we have to ensure we continue coaching the boys to a standard which gives them a great chance of realising their dreams. People shouldn't forget, though, that as well as being a great opportunity for the boys, it is a great

ABOVE: Liverpool's young goalkeepers are regularly put through their paces at the Academy.
OPPOSITE PAGE UPPER LEFT: Training inside the club's new state-of-the-art soccer hall.
LOWER LEFT: The youngsters enjoy the same kind of gymnasium facilities as the first team at Melwood.

opportunity for all the staff at the Academy to improve as well. This is a such a great place to work and we are all hopeful that many of the boys with us now will be challenging for the first team in years to come.'

Liverpool's record of producing players from their youth set-up is second to none. Robbie Fowler, Michael Owen, Steve McManaman, Jamie Carragher, David Thompson, Dominic Matteo and Steven Gerrard have all been brought through the ranks at Anfield and Reds supporters are desperately hoping there will be many more.

Frank Skelly, Liverpool's Youth Co-ordinator, believes the current crop of youngsters at the Academy have the potential to follow in the footsteps of their illustrious predecessors.

He says: 'The boys we bring to the Academy have to be the very best in their age group. Our standards are very high and we have a slogan entitled 'TABS'

which stands for 'Technique, Attitude, Balance, Speed'. Of course it is very hard to find a young boy who has all of these attributes – if we did then we would have a superstar on our hands – but we have to be sure that anyone who comes here has at least two of those qualities and then we can work with them on the other areas.

'When they are with us we don't just concentrate on their footballing skills because it is important they develop as young men as well. Social skills are also very important, as is their education, and that is why we insist that the boys continue with their education when they are with us. If they don't make it as a footballer then they have to have something to fall back on and we work very closely with the parents to make sure we are doing the best we possibly can for their children.

'We have classrooms at the Academy where lessons are given or where they

can do their homework and we give them all the support we possibly can. Of course young boys have personal problems whether they are with Liverpool or anywhere else and so we do our best to give them as much help as we can.

'As they are representing Liverpool it is important that they conduct themselves in the right manner. All sorts of sacrifices have to be made if you want to become a professional footballer but I think the boys feel that the sacrifices are well worth it if they realise their ambitions.'

A better break

Of course it is performances on the pitch which will ultimately decide whether the youngsters are destined for a career in football, and the recent changes to the set-up of youth football matches gives the players a better chance than ever of reaching the required standard.

Explains Frank: 'Before the start of last

ABOVE: The Liverpool coaching staff like to keep the training sessions fun as well as serious.

Weight training routines are crucial to young players as they build up their body strength.

ABOVE: Stretching is vital before any other sort of exercise.
BELOW: All the club's youngsters are regularly assessed as they continue to develop their body strength ready for the demands of competitive football.

season we were playing Lancashire League football but since the formation of the Academy League last year we are playing to a much higher standard. We have two teams – under-17 and under-19 – who both play on a Saturday morning or afternoon.

'Because we are now only playing against other sides who have an Academy we are competing against the stronger clubs which is good for our players because they will develop quicker. Last season was a good one for us and both of our teams fared reasonably well. We are hoping we can continue to improve this time around.

'The idea, of course, is to build players up to a standard whereby the first-team manager can take a look at them. Last season Steven Gerrard and Stephen Wright were both handed squad numbers just a few weeks into the new campaign and that was a tremendous boost to them as well as being an excellent endorsement of the work we are doing.

'Steven Gerrard is now a regular member of the first-team squad and he deserves it because of the work and effort he put in when he was with us. We hope there will be more to follow this season and there certainly are some youngsters who have made good progress. It isn't right to name players who we think could be next in line for the first-team squad because that puts unnecessary pressure on them, but the simple fact that they are with us says that we think they have something to offer. It is up to each individual to keep working hard because they have seen examples of what rewards can come their way.'

BELOW: Players and coach share a laugh.

- The Academy provides three weekly coaching sessions of two hours each for boys in the under-9s, under-10s, under-11s, under- 12s, under-13s, under-14s, under-15s and under-16s age categories and a game against another Academy on a Sunday.

- The synthetic surface, manufactured by Polytan, is the most advanced in the country, permitting full use of any boot or stud.

- Over five tonnes of grass was sown at the site and 12,500 metres of land drainage laid.

- The club sought permission from the Environment Agency to sink two 90-metre boreholes at the Academy to provide its own source of water for irrigation purposes. The water is stored in a 95,500-litre water tank.

- Over 110 tonnes of steel were used in the perimeter fencing of the site.

- The Academy was designed with local environmental needs in mind. All surface water from the site is stored in four underground storage tanks. Controlled pumping to Kirkby Brook can only take place when surrounding water levels have dropped to alleviate any danger of flooding the River Alt.

- The Academy has five full-time groundsmen, and two full-time physiotherapists along with a dedicated Academy doctor and a full-time education and welfare officer.

MATCH DAY

Training is over. Tactics have been
discussed. The team has been picked.
The players are ready and so are the fans…

YOU'LL NEVER WALK ALONE

LIVERPOOL
FOOTBALL CLUB

EST·1892 ®

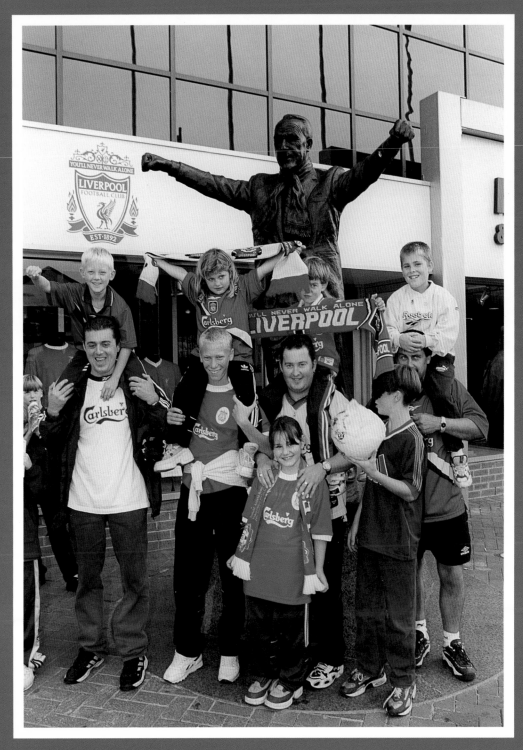

Happy fans stand outside the ground beneath the bronze statue of Bill Shankly.

Match Day at Anfield is a unique experience for the thousands of loyal football fans who fill it to capacity for every home game.

Regarded throughout the footballing world as one of the finest stadiums, the noise rolling down from the stands as kick-off approaches is enough to leave a lump in the throat of any supporter – even those who have experienced it many times before. For the youngsters among the 40,000-plus

TOP: Safety stewards have a morning briefing session on what to expect from the day's game.
ABOVE LEFT: Stadium manager Ged Poynton in discussion with the police prior to kick-off.
ABOVE RIGHT: Announcements can be made and the crowd monitored from the match control room.

crowd, the chance to see their heroes in action ensures a day of excitement they will never forget.

But there is much more to a match day at Anfield than the football between 3pm and 4.45pm. Days of planning go into the preparation for every game and there are far more people involved than just the footballers.

The safety and comfort of fans inside the stadium is always of paramount importance and will never be compromised. It is for that reason that so much meticulous planning goes into the policing of every match in the days and hours leading up to the kick-off.

Stadium Manager and Safety Certificate holder Ged Poynton explains: 'Before every game we have several meetings with the Merseyside police and we also liaise with the police force from the area of the opposing team so that we can identify any possible problems and gather intelligence. We leave nothing to chance. We have a de-briefing session before the game where we look at the events of the previous match and discuss any areas where improvements are necessary.

'The match day operation has been tried and tested many times over the years and we like to think we have got it about right. Depending on the size and scale of the game we may have to make one or two slight alterations but the basic operation remains the same. High-profile games sometimes bring different problems but we are always ready to deal with any incidents.

'Inside the stadium we have 30 cameras which constantly monitor the crowd. It is possible to focus in on any one person anywhere in the stadium thanks to the quality of the equipment we have. We can take a video or still photograph as well where

DIRECTORS AND OFFICIALS

Stewards on match day duty at the Main Reception.

necessary. Every steward on duty during a game knows what is expected of them.

'I have to say, though, that Liverpool fans are very well-behaved and we rarely encounter major problems. We are there to look after them and to make sure they are watching the match in a safe and comfortable environment.'

The turnstiles leading into the stadium open approximately one and a half hours before kick-off and, with each turnstile linked to a central computer, the number of fans inside the ground at any time can be counted.

Within an hour and a half the stadium is full to capacity and awaiting the entrance of the two teams on to the field. The players themselves usually arrive at the stadium little more than an hour before the kick-off. FA regulations stipulate that the referee should be in possession of the team sheet from both clubs 60 minutes before the game begins.

The Liverpool players travel to Anfield by coach after enjoying a pre-match meal at their Melwood training ground.

Most players have a particular favourite meal which they enjoy before every match while others chop and change from week to week.

Catering for everyone

The Melwood catering staff are instructed as to which foods are permitted on the menu to allow the players to perform to their full potential out on the field. There are two full-time canteen ladies at the training ground who prepare meals for the players on a daily basis after training and also before matches, when the players gather together for their last team meeting before heading to Anfield.

Chicken and pasta continue to be favourite meals for the majority of Liverpool players as professional footballers nowadays are more aware than ever before of the need to eat the right foods, designed to aid them on the field.

As the players are enjoying their light meals at Melwood, hundreds of people are taking advantage of Liverpool's excellent corporate hospitality within the stadium at Anfield.

The Liverpool FC match day programme is one of the best-selling in the premier league.

With executive boxes inside the stadium and many bars and lounges accommodating business people on a match day, the Anfield catering staff are kept extremely busy as they prepare hundreds of meals.

Head Chef Phil Rowlands explains: 'A match day is definitely the busiest time of the week for us. With 30 executive boxes along with numerous lounges and suites throughout the stadium, there are lots of people who we cater for.

'We provide meals for 1,600 customers on a Saturday and that size of operation requires a lot of pre-planning and preparation work. It takes about three days to organise a match day. If we are at home on the Saturday then our work begins on the previous Wednesday. That is when I get a list of what people in the executive boxes want to eat before the game and I put the order in accordingly. The food will usually arrive on the following day and then we go from there. Our menus vary throughout the year and we try to offer as many choices as possible.

'We have been doing this a long time now and so we know the procedure, but still our standards are high and we like to make sure that everyone who we cater for enjoys their day out at Anfield. Liverpool have a high reputation on the pitch and we try to ensure our reputation is equally as high off it.'

Although corporate hospitality continues to boom within football, Liverpool FC have never forgotten the importance of the fans who are catered for in the many refreshment areas around the stadium.

A busy place

Indeed, supporters have much to keep themselves busy ahead of the kick-off. Walking around the stadium before a game there are plenty of options to purchase all manner of goods ranging from traditional match day souvenirs to match programmes and club fanzines.

The Anfield match programme is usually printed a couple of days before the game to allow for any last-minute alterations. This season it has expanded to 64 pages and it is without doubt one of the best of its kind in the Premiership, illustrated by the fact that at nearly every game this season every programme printed has been sold.

If you are feeling lucky you can even buy a 'Golden Goal' ticket before the match with prizes to be won if your ticket matches the time of the first goal scored during the game.

Fans often take time out to remember the 96 people who lost their lives at Hillsborough as they flock to the memorial erected outside the Shankly Gates which has an everlasting flame burning in memory of the victims. It isn't just Liverpool scarves and flags adorning the memorial – souvenirs from other clubs are just as evident as a nation continues to remember the tragic events of ten years ago.

The huge Liverpool shop is extremely busy on match day as eager Liverpool fans look for the chance to snap up Anfield souvenirs, and the museum continues to be an extremely popular attraction for all who visit. With a detailed breakdown of the club's history as well as the chance to view priceless items of memorabilia from Liverpool's glorious past, the museum is a must-see attraction for all who visit Anfield. There is even the opportunity to test your soccer skills in an exciting shooting competition.

Business in the club shop is brisk on match day, but there's still time for a joke or two.

The players arrive

Once the players and management staff have made the short journey by coach from Melwood to Anfield they enter by the player's entrance on the Main Stand side of the ground. For security reasons they walk through a tunnelled area to get inside the stadium but there are still always hundreds of fans there to welcome them and wish them luck.

Once inside the stadium all the players have different pre-match routines. Some like to get themselves psyched up with exercises in the dressing room while others look for family and friends inside the ground to chat with. However, they all report back to the dressing room one hour before the kick-off for the final briefing from manager Gérard Houllier.

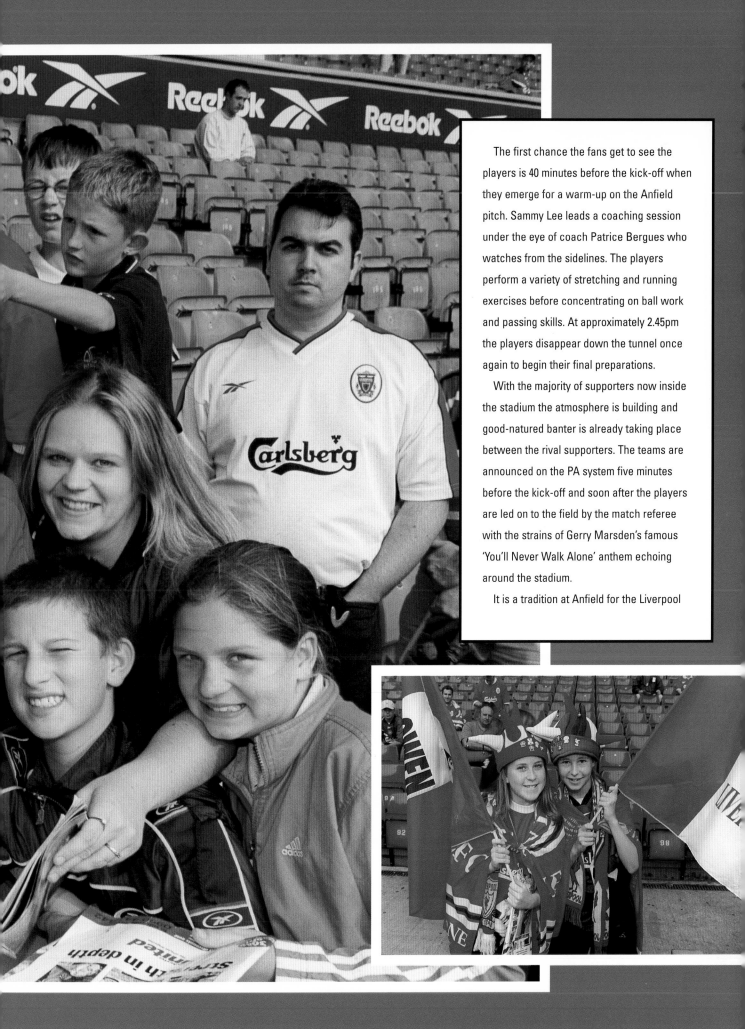

The first chance the fans get to see the players is 40 minutes before the kick-off when they emerge for a warm-up on the Anfield pitch. Sammy Lee leads a coaching session under the eye of coach Patrice Bergues who watches from the sidelines. The players perform a variety of stretching and running exercises before concentrating on ball work and passing skills. At approximately 2.45pm the players disappear down the tunnel once again to begin their final preparations.

With the majority of supporters now inside the stadium the atmosphere is building and good-natured banter is already taking place between the rival supporters. The teams are announced on the PA system five minutes before the kick-off and soon after the players are led on to the field by the match referee with the strains of Gerry Marsden's famous 'You'll Never Walk Alone' anthem echoing around the stadium.

It is a tradition at Anfield for the Liverpool

squad members to touch the 'This is Anfield' sign which greets the players as they enter the field. It was an idea of Bill Shankly's that the sign would intimidate the opposition before they had even kicked off.

Of course the media play an increasingly important role in the modern game, as it is their views that the supporters will be reading in the newspapers in the days following the match. The press are assembled in the Main Stand where journalists from the press and radio prepare to comment. Television camera crews are housed on the gantry which is suspended from the roof of the Main Stand. That is where TV commentators also broadcast their match commentaries from.

During a match most eyes inside the stadium will of course be on the action, but there are some people who are unfortunate enough not to see a ball being kicked. Match stewards are there to watch the crowd and not to see the football. They have a duty to help maintain crowd control and crowd safety. Security stewards continue to patrol the doors of the stadium during a game while the club's receptionists take a well-earned breather after what is usually a hectic build-up to the game.

The day is done

Once the match has finished and the crowd leave, the clear-up operation has to begin. 'I am never happy until the last fan has left the stadium in a safe manner,' says Ged Poynton. 'It is only then that I can relax and begin to plan for the next game.'

As the fans leave, talking about the match and about individual performances, the press prepare for the thoughts of the two managers about the game. Approximately half an hour after the final whistle Gérard Houllier will emerge to discuss his thoughts in the press room, while a couple of players are asked for their comments as they make their way to the players' lounge to meet up with their families after matches. The result usually determines whether the players are in the mood to talk – sometimes disappointment leaves them feeling as if talking is the last thing they want to do.

While match analysis is taking place inside the corridors of Anfield, out on the pitch the ground staff are already beginning to repair the damage caused to the surface during the game. Head groundsman Reg Summers says: 'We usually leave the majority of the repair work until the day after the game when we repair the divots and mow the surface in readiness for the next game. During a match I am watching to see how the pitch is playing. The work we carry out at Anfield is on display for everybody to see and I think the management team are quite happy with the way the pitch has been playing of late.'

The club employs a team of cleaners to tidy the stadium after a match while the Anfield maintenance team begins to assess what damage, if any, was caused to seats or other items during the game.

The players usually leave the stadium more than an hour after the final whistle where they are always greeted by fanatical supporters who have waited, whatever the weather, to catch a glimpse of their heroes and, if they are lucky, to get a cherished autograph.

Then follows the journey home to all parts of Britain, and even Europe, for the supporters who continue to give their all in support of the club, week after week. The result often determines the mood of the fans as they make the trek home, but they always leave in the knowledge that they have experienced the thrill of a match day adventure at one of the most revered football grounds in the world.

QUIZZES

Test your knowledge of Liverpool Football Club past and present. There are questions for everyone – from those who joined in the summer to regulars celebrating their half-century of support for the Reds. Good luck, and you'll find the answers on page 96.

EASY

1   Against which team did Robbie Fowler score his first Liverpool goal?

2   Who succeeded Bob Paisley as Liverpool manager?

3   Who did Liverpool beat in the 1995 Coca-Cola Cup Final at Wembley?

4   Who scored both of Liverpool's goals on that afternoon?

5   From which club did Liverpool sign goalkeeper Sander Westerveld?

6   How many French-born players are on the books at Liverpool?

7   How many Liverpool players scored a goal in the last World Cup?

8   What was significant about Jamie Redknapp's Liverpool debut?

9   Of all Liverpool's summer signings, how many have previous Premiership experience?

10 What is the nationality of reserve goalkeeper Jorgen Nielsen?

Name the player – he was a star at Euro '96 in England.

Name the player – one of Liverpool's favourite strikers.

Name the player – he left Liverpool in September 1999.

Name the player – the one on the right – without looking up his number, if you can.

MEDIUM

1   Against which country did Michael Owen make his England debut?

2   What is the fewest number of goals conceded by Liverpool in a League season?

3   What is Liverpool's longest unbeaten League sequence?

4   Which player has made the most appearances for Liverpool in total?

5   Against which team did Robbie Fowler score his first Liverpool hat-trick?

6   Who missed Liverpool's penalty in the 1984 European Cup final shoot-out with AS Roma?

7   And who scored the four Liverpool spot-kicks in that same penalty competition?

8   From which club did Liverpool sign midfielder John Wark?

9   Who was the last player to play for both Liverpool and Everton?

10 Who knocked Liverpool out of last season's Worthington Cup?

A

Name the player – he's currently one of the longest-serving names at the club.

B

How many times was Bob Paisley named Manager of the Year?

C

Which club did this player leave to join Liverpool?

D

Name the player – he went to play in London after Liverpool.

DIFFICULT

1   Against which team did Liverpool play in Bill Shankly's first match
        as manager?

2   Which former Liverpool player was featured on the cover of the
        famous Beatles album *Sergeant Pepper's Lonely Hearts Club Band*?

3   How many times have Liverpool been relegated from the top flight?

4   Which was the first team to win against Liverpool at Anfield in the
        European Cup?

5   How many Russian teams have knocked Liverpool out of European
        competition?

6   Of Liverpool's 15 FA Cup Final goals, what is different about
        Hunt's in 1965 and Case's in 1977?

7   Which former Liverpool player was also a junior volleyball
        international?

8   Against which team did Robbie Fowler score his 50th
        Liverpool goal?

9   Liverpool lost three games in a row last season at Anfield – against
        which sides?

10   Which Liverpool favourite of the Eighties and Nineties is now
        managing in US Major League Soccer?

Name the player – having some alternative physiotherapy.

What was the date of this game?

Name the player – when did he play his first Liverpool vs. Everton match?

Name the player – what was the final score in this game?

ANSWERS

EASY QUESTIONS

1 Fulham
2 Joe Fagan
3 Bolton
4 Steve McManaman
5 Vitesse Arnhem in Holland
6 One – Djimi Traore
7 One – Michael Owen (against Romania and Argentina)
8 He became the youngest player to ever play for Liverpool in European competition
9 Two – Stephane Henchoz and Dietmar Hamann
10 Danish

A Patrik Berger
B Robbie Fowler
C Karlheinz Riedle
D Jamie Carragher

MEDIUM QUESTIONS

1 Chile
2 16 in season 1978–79
3 31 matches
4 Ian Callaghan – 640 between 1960 and 1978
5 Fulham in a 5–0 win (he scored all five)
6 Steve Nicol
7 Phil Neal, Graeme Souness, Ian Rush and Alan Kennedy
8 Ipswich Town
9 Don Hutchison
10 Tottenham Hotspur

A Jamie Redknapp
B Six
C Skelmersdale United
D Neil Ruddock

DIFFICULT QUESTIONS

1 Cardiff City on December 19, 1959. Cardiff won 4–0
2 Albert Stubbins
3 Three times. In seasons 1894–95, 1903–04 and 1953–54
4 Ferencvaros of Hungary by one goal to nil in January 1968
5 Two – Spartak Moscow and Dynamo Tblisi
6 They were the only goals scored at the tunnel end of Wembley
7 Alan Hansen
8 Tottenham Hotspur
9 Derby County, Tottenham Hotspur and Leeds United
10 Steve Nicol

A Vladimir Smicer
B September 27, 1996
C Alec Lindsay – November 21, 1970
D Mark Wright – Paris St-Germain 3–0 Liverpool